CONFESSIONS OF A FOOTBALL

Contents

CONFESSIONS OF A FOOTBALL CHAPLAIN

FOREWORD BY CRAIG BROWN CBE

Having worked for more than 60 years in the professional game, all that is written in this thoroughly captivating book resonates perfectly with me.

Author, Mark Fleming, cogently shares about his experience as chaplain to *three* football clubs. Over the years I had the privilege of being signed as a player by three clubs in Scotland – Rangers, Dundee and Falkirk. I managed three Scottish clubs – Clyde, Motherwell and Aberdeen and three clubs south of the border – Preston North End, Fulham and Derby County. The similarities don't end there though, as Mark and I have both enjoyed working with the Scottish FA, in my case, for 15 years. I can personally confirm that Mark has accurately managed to encapsulate all that makes engrossment in football such an appealing experience.

I have had the privilege of associating with several high quality football club chaplains, including the author. My introduction to football chaplaincy was while assistant manager of Motherwell in the mid-1970s when Rev Jimmy Martin was the popular chaplain at the Fir Park Club. It was very much an informal role then with Jimmy. Like Mark at Partick Thistle, Jimmy joined in training sessions but, unlike Mark (sorry Sir!), played very well. There invariably is much jocular banter among players and Jimmy's presence tended to exacerbate that situation because everyone wanted to be in the Rev's side in the fun, small-sided game, which concluded most training sessions. If you were in "God's Pal's" team it was considered a major advantage and everyone on his side pointed Heavenwards when they scored a goal!

One of the former chaplains I worked with was Rev Chris Nelson at Preston North End. Chris had a wide range of skillsets, which equipped him to deal with situations ranging from dealing with a player's starving dog (alluded to later in the book) and his delivering a wonderful and emotional eulogy at the remarkable funeral of 91 year old Sir Tom Finney CBE, arguably one of the finest English players ever.

Players, even at the top level, often require reassurance, encouragement and confidential help. In providing such assistance, the chaplain invariably develops a close relationship with his 'football flock'. An example of this relates to the experience of current Hibernian Sporting Director, Graeme Mathie. When playing for Bournemouth, he developed a great affinity with the club chaplain, Rev Alan Fisher, who officiated at Graeme's wedding. The Scottish player asked what he could do to reciprocate Alan's support. The chaplain replied, "Please say a few words at my funeral. In English though, if you speak Scottish no one will understand you!" When the elderly chaplain died, age 92 in 2016, Mr Mathie spoke eloquently, in English, as requested.

One of Mark Fleming's foremost tasks relates to recruitment. In this regard he is unvaryingly on the ball. This was definitely the case at Aberdeen because after very little discussion, Barry Douglas was identified as the perfect candidate. Barry did not get off to a good start, as Aberdeen lost at home to Motherwell. After the final whistle, Barry was told by Stewart Milne, the then Chairman, that he would have to improve his performance. Now, doesn't the chaplain get blamed for everything?

The role of the club chaplain is, unsurprisingly, to develop fine relationships with all staff and not just the players. Confidentiality is of paramount importance but it is widely known that the chaplain has to deal with police cases, suicide, depression, gambling, mental health issues – in addition to officiating at private family ceremonies. These intimate, trusting relationships only confirm the status of the chaplain in the players' lounge. This kudos has been confirmed by the fact that during Barry's time at Aberdeen three players have asked him to conduct their weddings – Josh Magennis, Peter Pawlett and Curtis Main.

Mark has most certainly scored a winner with this unique, insightful, and amusing narrative. It is a fascinating read with either a 'Lambieism' or a deleted expletive to provide even greater authenticity. In Mark's self-effacing manner he credits the late legend John Lambie for being significant in the development of Sports Chaplaincy Scotland. I, therefore, indirectly also owe a debt to John, my former teammate at Falkirk, because I now have the honour of being Patron of Sports Chaplaincy Scotland.

CONFESSIONS OF A FOOTBALL CHAPLAIN

INTRODUCTION

My earliest childhood memory is when I was four years old. I was visiting my grandparents, who lived in an apartment on the second floor of an old tenement building in Leyden Gardens, Maryhill, in the North of Glasgow. I stood beside my Grandpa in his kitchen and asked him, "Grandpa, what team do you support?" He gazed out of the kitchen window, pointed in the direction of Firhill Road, and said, "There's only one team in Glasgow, son! The locals - Partick Thistle!"

I believed him, and despite discovering that there were, in fact, other teams in the city, I remained convinced that there really was only one team in Glasgow worth supporting. That was the Jags, the Harry Wraggs, the Maryhill Magyars – a comparison with the immensely talented Hungarian national football team of the 1950s.

In 1971, on my eighth birthday, I received my first ever replica Partick Thistle top. It was a beautiful yellow colour, with a kind of orangey tint, and a red trim. Whatever everyone else may have thought of its aesthetic qualities, it will go down in history as the most famous Jags top. This is because, two weeks previously, on 23 October, Thistle had arguably caused the greatest Cup upset of all time in Scotland. They defeated the mighty Glasgow Celtic 4-1 in the Scottish League Cup final.

On that momentous day, Sam Leitch, who was a presenter on the BBC Saturday sports program Grandstand, is quoted as saying, "In Scotland, it's League Cup final day at Hampden Park, where Celtic meet Partick

Thistle, who have no chance." To be fair to Sam, most people in Scotland would have agreed with him.

Partick Thistle had just been promoted to the top division and Celtic had appeared in the 1970 European Cup Final. With players like Kenny Dalglish, Jimmy Johnstone and Lou Macari, surely Celtic only had to turn up to receive the trophy? Maybe that is what some of their players thought because Thistle were 4-0 up after only 37 minutes, and the score remained the same going into half-time.

One of my great Firhill friends, the Club historian Robert Reid, is well known for his pessimism and, at the interval, he was considering just how humiliating it would be for Celtic to win 5-4, perhaps sharing Sam's doubts. Although Kenny Dalglish did pull a goal back for the Hoops, Thistle did not capitulate. On that day, there really was only one team in Glasgow! Well, you didn't think I would write a book with any reference to the Jags without mentioning the 4-1 game did you?

Apart from that famous victory about 50 years ago, why on earth would anyone support Partick Thistle when there are two much bigger and more successful football clubs in the same city? Well, apart from not simply wanting to go along with crowd, it's fair to say that there is baggage with Rangers and Celtic. The majority of their fans are decent people. However, both clubs have sections of their support who have been guilty of sectarianism. But Partick Thistle? They are the "Great Glasgow Alternative". An alternative to bigotry, glory-hunting, sheep-following, large intimidating crowds – and yes to success, championships and cups too, but it's a price Jags fans are willing to pay – just to be different!

Like many other young boys growing up in Scotland, I would have loved to have become a professional footballer. And Partick Thistle was the only one club I would have wanted to play for. However, there were a few factors that put me at a disadvantage. For one I was very overweight as a child – my nickname at school was Flabby. Secondly, I wore glasses. Thirdly, I was not the most talented player you have ever seen. In fact, I was usually last pick in the playground.

My only success as a young footballer was captaining a five-a-side team that reached the semi-finals of a tournament in which I earned a "player of the tournament" award. You may be wondering how wee Flabby Fleming led his team to the semi-finals? Easy, only four teams entered that particular age-group competition. And the "player of the tournament"? Well, to be more accurate, the full title of my accolade was "*most enthusiastic* player of the tournament". I'll take that! What I lacked in skill I certainly made up for in enthusiasm. In the solitary game we played, we were 4-0 down, and I scored a consolation goal. I celebrated like we had won the World Cup. I would have lifted my jersey over my head in celebration but I had struggled to put it on over my tubby frame before the game so I was concerned that I might get it stuck over my head. This would have led to me running around like a headless chicken for the rest of the game. To be honest, it would not have made much difference because that's what I was doing anyway.

CONFESSIONS OF A FOOTBALL CHAPLAIN

I have no doubt that excess weight and limited eyesight would have contributed to my lack of footballing prowess. However, I lost all that puppy fat and became fit and healthy. I could have got contact lenses. The fact still remained – I did not have sufficient talent to ever think about playing football for a living – I struggled to get a game for an amateur team. That did not stop me from loving football and Partick Thistle in particular.

I have never understood supporters who think that paying money to attend a football match gives them the right to abuse players, managers and directors. And I could not see how being verbally abused and threatened with violence would *not* adversely affect people involved in football. In the 1980s, Thistle had a left back called Bobby Law. He had a powerful strike with his left foot that could end up in either the top corner of the net or a street corner in nearby Possilpark. But the one thing Bobby always gave was a wholehearted performance. I remember reading a match day programme article that featured him and he was asked the question, "What is your ambition here at Firhill?" His answer actually saddened me and I have never forgotten it: "To enjoy playing my football again here." The joy of playing football had left him, largely due to the verbal abuse he used to get off some so-called supporters.

I was not like the "boo boys". Sure, there were occasions when I was frustrated and upset but I always felt the players were doing their best. They were not intentionally conceding goals, failing to score or win games. I continued to support my beloved Jags through thick and thin. There was nothing more I could do. Was there?

I was about to discover that there *was* something I could do. And not only would this help my club, it would ultimately have a positive effect on Scottish football as a whole.

CHAPTER 1

SAVE THE JAGS

Given my love for the club, like many others, the prospect of Partick Thistle FC going out of business was simply unthinkable. Yet, in 1998, that is exactly what could have happened. However, the "Save the Jags" campaign was started by the fans to raise funds in order to keep the club alive. At the forefront of this great effort was Allan Cowan. I knew Allan well, having grown up in the same village – Fairlie, near Largs. I am quite sure he never anticipated the level of involvement that this fundraising venture would lead him to have with the club or all the hassle that goes with it. Allan became a director and then Chairman before going back to simply being a fan again.

I had conducted his sister Mairi's wedding atop the Munro mountain, Stob Ghabar, and the reception was held a week later to enable us to recover from our climb and enjoy the ceilidh. I chatted to Allan at the reception and asked how he was getting on since becoming a director at Thistle. He told me that because of the ongoing financial uncertainty, the players were struggling to focus on football – they had wives, families, mortgages and other financial responsibilities. The manager felt more like a social worker or counsellor than a football coach. He was trying to prepare them for a game each Saturday in order to help them survive in the second tier of Scottish senior football. The players were more concerned about how they would survive in the practicalities of everyday life, never mind the First Division!

As Allan told me this, it occurred to me that maybe I could be of service to the club. I may not have had a great left foot but I could offer a listening ear. I could possibly give wise counsel if required. Fans are generally oblivious to the pressures the chairman, directors, administration staff, manager and players face off the park, they are usually only concerned about what is achieved on the park. However, if matters are not right off the park, chances are they will have an adverse effect on what happens on the park. So I offered my services as a chaplain. I did not have a clear idea what I was actually offering, and neither did Allan, but I wanted to do my bit to "save the Jags".

A few days later, I received a phone call from someone claiming to be a reporter from the Glasgow Evening Times. He told me his name was Graham Scott and said, "I understand you have been appointed as chaplain to Partick Thistle, could we have an interview?" At that stage, I had not heard back from Allan Cowan or anyone else from Partick Thistle about my offer to become chaplain. Convinced that one of my friends was winding me up, I replied, "Aye sure mate and I'm going to be the next Pope too!" The caller tried to assure me that he was a genuine reporter but I was having none of it. He suggested that I call up the Sports Desk at the Evening Times and ask to speak to the senior sports reporter, Graham Scott, to assuage my scepticism. I called his bluff. I looked up the Yellow Pages, phoned up the newspaper, asked for the Sports Desk and then for Graham Scott – and to my great embarrassment found myself speaking to said caller again! This is what happens to people who love to wind up their friends – it eventually comes back to bite you, even with false teeth.

Maybe I should give you an example of why I thought it might be someone pulling my leg... Shortly before this embarrassment, I had been in a meeting with other local church pastors. I told one of my colleagues that a woman I knew was desperate to come to his church because where she attended at present "did not have much life about it". I gave him her office phone number and told him he would have to ask for her, using her full name, as there were several people in the company for which she worked who were called by the same forename – Myra. I suggested that he call her from the office we were meeting in while the rest of us waited outside, to give him some privacy. However, I confess that I left the door slightly ajar, so that I and my other colleagues could listen in. Here is how the telephone conversation went:

"Hello, can I speak to Myra Mains please?"

"I think someone is taking the **** sir."

"No, that was definitely her name – can I have Myra Mains please?"

"Sir, this is Paisley Crematorium."

Meanwhile, we were collapsing on the floor laughing. Well, I did tell him that the place Myra was in "did not have much life about it"! And that is just one reason why I did not believe it was really Graham Scott from the Evening Times. But it was.

From Partick Thistle's perspective, this is the account of my appointment: After Allan had talked to me at his sister's wedding reception, he brought the suggestion of appointing a chaplain to the club's next board meeting. The chairman, Brown McMaster, was a genuine and caring family man. He liked the idea of pastoral support being made available to everyone at the club. However, he was also conscious of the club's financial constraints due to their recent crisis. He was understandably concerned about how much this new service would cost the club. Allan reassured Brown and the rest of the board, "Oh it's okay, it's Mark, he's a Jags fan, he'll do it for free!" His assumption was accurate. I was more than happy to offer my services to Partick Thistle, without incurring any cost to the club. This remains part of the DNA of Sports Chaplaincy Scotland today – all of our chaplains are staff volunteers. This helps us retain our neutrality and objectivity. It also means that when a club is forced to take cost-cutting measures, they do not need to dispense with the services of their chaplain.

The board agreed to my appointment and informed the Evening Times of their "new signing". On reflection, it might have been a good idea for Thistle to let me know too, saving me the embarrassment of that phone call exchange with Graham Scott!

I was officially announced as club chaplain on 22 July 1998. The following month I was due to move from Paisley to become senior pastor at Kilsyth Community Church. Given the time commitment that was going to be required from me in my role as a football club chaplain – Friday from 9am to 2pm and most Saturday afternoons for games – I felt I should check with the church leaders that they were happy with this arrangement. They could not have been more supportive. They wanted me to consider it as part of my working week and even insisted on covering my travel expenses. They thought that being a football chaplain would be a good release for me from the pressures of local church ministry. Over the years that followed, the church continued to be a great encouragement to me as Sports Chaplaincy Scotland was birthed and developed. The church eventually paid the ultimate price for their support 16 years later when I stepped down as pastor in order to work full-time with Sports Chaplaincy Scotland. But I am way ahead of myself, let's go back to the beginning!

Tommy Bryce was the manager of Partick Thistle when I started at Firhill. It was his first and his last foray into senior club management. He was great with me, even though the concept of chaplaincy was completely new to him. He suggested that I train with the players so that I could get to know them better – this certainly helped keep me humble. One evening after training, a Roman Catholic player, Des McKeown, said to me, "Rev, I don't know what your version of a novena is but you'd better say one for a first touch, yours is ******* terrible!" At the time I was crestfallen, until it occurred to me that this was a sign that I was being accepted. You know you are part of the group when everyone feels free to laugh at you! If you want to be a chaplain, you cannot afford to take yourself too seriously. You have to be able to laugh at yourself because everyone else is probably going to…

CONFESSIONS OF A FOOTBALL CHAPLAIN

After a sticky start to the season, a 3-2 loss to East Fife in the League Cup and a 1-0 league defeat to Inverness Caledonian Thistle, we went on a great run – six wins and a draw. Given the famed inconsistency of Thistle, this bordered on the miraculous! Indeed, one of the directors, who claimed to be an atheist, came up to me and declared that it must have been because the club had appointed a chaplain that the team was doing so well – at long last God was clearly on our side! I was quick to point out that I was not a witchdoctor, that my presence and influence had not led to these great results – it was purely down to the management and players' performances. I am so glad that I did not take any of the credit – we lost eight of the next nine games. Poor Tommy was sacked on 6 March 1999, after five consecutive defeats. If my role had been perceived to be in any way performance-related, I would have been out of the door with him!

I strongly advise our chaplains to never take the credit for success so they will not receive the blame for failure. Over the years, when results have not been going Thistle's way, people have often joked with me that it was my fault because I did not pray hard enough. Believe me, if praying for victory was a legitimate aspect of chaplaincy, Thistle would have won the UEFA Champions League by now, never mind the Scottish Premiership! But it does not work that way. And therein lies one of the first principles of chaplaincy – our role is really to help people in the game have a successful life *off* the pitch.

To illustrate what a chaplain is not, I share the following story. The Netherlands were due to play Spain in the final of the 2010 World Cup.

Father Paul Vlaar made headlines when he celebrated mass wearing an orange cassock, the colour of the Dutch national team, sang an orange song and decorated the church with football flags. In the West of Scotland, where I was raised, we would probably consider this the ultimate irony – a Roman Catholic priest singing an Orange song... you just could not script that! Anyway, in his prayer, he asked for solidarity and team spirit in the Dutch team. The outcome? He was suspended by the bishop for two months "for reflection"! His prayers were not very fruitful either. The Netherlands were defeated 1-0 by Spain, they had two players sent off in the process – and it soon became apparent that there was rather a lot of disunity in the camp too.

The chaplain is not there to effect team performances but to positively impact the personal lives of those involved in the game. We care more for people's souls than we do for goals. But if we are being honest, we do care about goals too!

When I first started as Thistle chaplain, my daughters were nine and seven respectively. They occasionally came to matches with me. However, it was not to sample the delights of the beautiful game – it was to sample the sweeties that Uncle Walter gave them. Walter Horner sat nearby me, he became a good friend and was the main reason why my girls came to the games. The ultimate sweetener.

My daughters could not understand why Thistle results affected my mood so much. So, they eventually decided to cash in on my fluctuating emotions. They announced they were going to fine me 50p every

Saturday night that I came in the door with a long face after a poor result. During the half hour drive home from Firhill I would do everything possible to psych myself up into a good mood. I would walk in the door attempting to display a huge smile regardless of the result. But every time they would say, "Dad, we saw the result, don't act it, we know you'll be gutted tonight – just give us the 50p now and be done with it!" Honestly, they made a pile of money from me. Desperate to try and claim back some of my lost fortune, I came up with a good counter-idea. I handed them a fine of 50p every time they left a light on in their bedroom, which they were continually doing, so I think I managed to balance the books on that score. After all, business is business! But that's not all – at the beginning of the season they would say, "Dad, see if Thistle get promotion this season, can we have a wee cash bonus from you to celebrate?" Chancers! Of course I agreed…

Thankfully, my dog Sweep was a lot more understanding and compassionate than my daughters. Dogs are amazing animals – so sensitive to your feelings! Recently I was telling a friend that when the results were announced on Sportscene on a Saturday afternoon, our Sweep would listen to the TV. If he heard the phrase, "Partick Thistle nil…" he would howl the place down. Incredible empathy! My friend asked me what Sweep's response was when Thistle won and I said, "I don't know, we only had him for six months!" Well I'm used to being the butt of peoples' jokes for being a Jags fan so I thought I would get in there first this time.

Back to chaplaincy at Partick Thistle.   When Tommy was sacked, Sammy Johnston and Willie Jamieson stepped up to the plate to take temporary charge. Thankfully, they were absolutely fine with me staying on as chaplain. At the end of their short tenure, I thanked them both for continuing to allow me to train with the players and Willie's words to me were, "You weren't the worst Rev!" A high compliment indeed from the man who scored one of the best goals I have seen in Scottish football. Yes, I'm talking about Willie Jamieson, the big Hearts central defender. It was in a game against Celtic in 1995. Willie was maybe about 35 yards out. When the Celtic players saw that the ball was at Willie's feet, it looked like they were not too concerned because no one closed him down. Maybe they thought that if he took a shot it was more likely to end up in Edinburgh Castle than in the back of the net. Wallop! Right in to the top corner. A stoater. So Willie knew a player when he saw one! Okay, he was just being kind to me.

Partick Thistle had been starved of major success for some time. Davie MacParland led them to *that* famous 4-1 League Cup final victory in 1971 against the mighty Celtic. Have I mentioned that before? Bertie Auld had led them to the Premier League in 1976. Since then, only one manager had enjoyed any notable success at Firhill – the legendary John Lambie. John was there from 1988 to 1989, then came back from 1990 to 1995. In his second spell, he led the club to the Premier League and kept them there throughout his tenure.

And the word on the street was – he was coming back!

CHAPTER 2

JOHN LAMBIE – THE GAFFER

To be honest, I was terrified at the prospect of John Lambie coming in as the new manager! I thought he would tell me where to go, and I don't mean in order to find the dressing room. Instead, I will never forget my first meeting with John in March 1999. In the foyer of the Main Stand before his first game in charge, Allan Cowan simply introduced me to him as the club chaplain. John shook my hand and then kissed my ring. I wasn't sure if he had mistook me for someone else of higher ecclesiastical standing! He said he was delighted the club had a chaplain as he was a great believer in God and thought I would be a great asset to the club. He said he would give me a personal introduction to the players before training the following Friday. Here is how that official introduction went:

"Right boys, this is an important person at this club. He's Mark, the club chaplain. So, see if you've any ******* problems, don't ******* come to me – ******* go to ******* him!" With that, he walked out of the dressing room and left me to it. What an introduction!

A few years later, I gave an interview to Radio Scotland, which was recorded and then aired at a later stage. I shared this story but, instead of swearing as John had done, I actually said "beeping" so that listeners would get the picture. However, when Radio Scotland aired the interview, they put actual beeps over my "beepings", which made it sound like I had been swearing like a trooper on national radio. I received a few phone calls after that from people expressing their concern about John's influence over my language!

What was fascinating about John was that he never swore in front of my wife, Aileen. There was one occasion when he came to our house for dinner with a couple of former players. While the four of us were eating dinner together, John's language was impeccable. However, after eating, Aileen left us to talk football and went to sit in the lounge next door. She was barely over the threshold when John started using a torrent of expletives as he reminisced about a particular footballing scenario. From the lounge, Aileen gently castigated our guest, "Em, John I can still hear you through here…" He replied, "Oh sorry hen, sorry hen!" and went back to speaking in perfect Queen's English – well maybe that's a bit of an exaggeration…

There are many wonderful stories to tell about John. One of my favourites is the time when we were travelling back from Inverness on the team bus after a match there. A few of the lads were playing a game, "Desert Island" where you tell the group who you would like to be alone with on a desert island. The category they were now on to was "beautiful women". Danny Lennon chose Kylie Minogue, Alan Archibald went for Beyoncé and Martin Hardie went for Danni Minogue. During the discussion, John came up the bus on his way to the toilet. Danny said, "Gaffer, we're playing a game. 'Who would you like to be stuck on a desert island with?' What about you?"

John replied, "My brother Duncan."

"No, no, no, Gaffer, you don't understand, we're talking about beautiful women – I'm going for Kylie, Archie's gone for Beyonce and Martin's gone for Danni Minogue."

"Nup, still would be my brother Duncan."

"But why Gaffer?"

Quick as a flash, John replies, "Cos I'd hate to be stuck on a ******* island and my brother Duncan has a ******* boat!"

Of course, I was not personally involved in a lot of the stories I could tell you about John Lambie, but they are worth the telling anyway! In 1974, when John was playing for St Johnstone, he decided that, although he loved his two girls, Janet and Isobel, he wanted to try for a boy. So he thought of a unique way to facilitate the conception of a male offspring. He dressed for action in his Saints football shorts, top, scarf and bunnet to perform his marital duties with his wife, Mamie. It did not work but any initial disappointment that he had another daughter very soon dissipated – because Carole was the golden girl, "the spoilt one". She had her dad wrapped around her little finger and then some!

I do not think any player who played under John Lambie ever had the leverage that Carole had. On one occasion, he fined Gerry Britton and George Shaw £50 each for a misdemeanour but gave them the option of buying him a nice bottle of whisky. Given their meagre wages at that time, Gerry did not want to incur such an expense. So, he emptied what was left of a bottle out of his dad's whisky collection and filled it with cold tea. Gerry and George presented John with this bottle of "whisky." A few weeks went by and it looked like they had managed to fool the manager as he had not said anything. But one day John invited a friend round who was a prominent local councillor and he opened this special bottle just for him. Needless to say, the boys were called into his office the next morning, and fined £100 each. You could not win with him.

Another time they were down in Blackpool staying at Norbreck Castle, which looked a bit like the Royal Infirmary in Glasgow. At the same time, a pigeon convention was being held in Blackpool. Funny how these trips often used to coincide... John had been drinking to considerable excess. Gerry started banging on John's door and then he moved a big wardrobe with its door open so that when John opened his door he walked right into the pitch black wardrobe, and he could be heard shouting, "Where the **** am I? Let me out, where the **** am I?" Gerry thought this was hilarious until five minutes later when John stormed into his room with a bucket of water, threw it over him and his bed, and said, "Right you, get all the players on the beach in 10 minutes." This was at 6am in mid-January and he had them running on the beach, while John was still considerably under the influence of alcohol!

He certainly knew how to motivate players. Before a game against Rangers, he gave all of the team a glass of champagne to help allay their nerves and, after George Shaw put them 1-0 up, it had seemed to work. They could probably have done with another glass as they were defeated 4-1.

It was not unknown for John to give his players something like a wee dram of whisky at half-time. On one occasion when they came in at the interval 2-0 down, he gave them a thimble-full of a drink which no one could identify. It was absolutely disgusting. One brave player asked, "Gaffer, what is this stuff? It's pure mingin'!" John replied, "It's new pigeon feed, I wanted to see if it made you lot any faster before I gave it to them!"

There are many famous sayings that we call "Lambieisms". I have heard a number of them first-hand: "My blood pressure is through the moon"; "Ach, we shot ourselves in the arm in that game."; "See you three, ya pair of *******"; "Our first goal was pure textile"; and, "Our defence couldnae keep weans out of a close".

John Lambie was an absolute delight to work with. His man-management skills were tremendous. He was a clever tactician and a brilliant motivator. If the impression you have of him is that he just shouted and swore at players, think again – he knew how to bring the best out of them. Although, don't think you could ever pull the wool over his eyes. One of my best pals at the club was Scott McLean, affectionately nicknamed "Trigger", after the character in Only Fools and Horses. He would do some of the daftest things but don't let that fool you – Scott is very intelligent. Unfortunately, that did not stop him from getting into a fair amount of trouble with John Lambie. While on holiday with the players in Ayia Napa at the end of the previous season, Scott had met a lovely girl called Rachel. Even though Rachel lived in Coventry, Scott tried to see her as often as possible. After playing on one particular Saturday, he went off down south that evening to spend a few days with her. The only problem with that was he was supposed to be at training on Monday morning and was due to play in a game the following night. When there was no sign of him at training on the Monday, the manager sent Davie, the club's masseur, round to Scott's apartment. After a while, it was clear that Davie was wasting his time, there was no answer. So, John called Scott on his mobile phone. Here is how the conversation went:

"Trigger, where the f*** are you?"

Thinking on his feet, well actually lying in Rachel's bed, "Gaffer, I'm really struggling. I've got a terrible dose of the flu…"

"Is that right Trigger, well Davie's round at your flat to check on you. Let him in!"

"Gaffer, honestly, I'm that ill, I can't even get out of my bed. I'm in a bad way!"

"I'll tell you why you ******** can't answer the ******* door to Davie. Cos you're not ******* there, you're in ******* Coventry and when I get my ******** hands on you…"

I saw Scott as a wee brother, I was always looking out for him. One day I could tell he was struggling to fit his contact lenses so I asked him if he was okay. "Och, not really Rev. I use daily lenses, only I'm a bit skint just now, so I've got to use the same daily lense for four days at a time." I was horrified, concerned that he might damage his eyes. I had a friend,

Dougie, who worked for Specsavers so I phoned him and asked if he was interested in a good PR exercise, "How would you feel about sponsoring my pal with free daily contact lenses for a year if I can get you a story on the back page of the Evening Times?" He was up for it so I contacted my friend at the newspaper, Graham Scott, and he was happy to do the business. Scott was able to see clearly for a whole year after that!

Scott was one of my daughters' favourite players. However, it was nothing to do with what he produced on the pitch. It was about what he produced when he visited our house – Scott would always bring a bag of Cadbury's chocolate buttons for both of my wee girls. After he moved on from Thistle I still kept in touch with him but we did not see him at the house for about eight years. When he returned to see us, my girls were now both in their mid-teens – but much to their amusement Scott still brought them chocolate buttons. He had a shocked look on his face as he said, "Oh no, I forgot you would've grown up by now! I was still thinking you were wee girls!" Not that they were complaining though, who doesn't love chocolate buttons?

John was happy for me to continue training with the players every Friday morning so that I could get to know them and build relationships of trust. This meant I needed training gear. Two of the best signings John Lambie ever made were that of the two kit men, Ricky and Chico. They were two of the funniest guys I have ever met – integral to life at Partick Thistle and they left a huge gap when they died within a short time of each other in recent years. They gave me my own kit, with the initials

CONFESSIONS OF A FOOTBALL CHAPLAIN

REV printed on the front of the training top and shorts. Just as the players have their names printed on the back of their shirts, my training top received the same treatment. Except in my case Ricky and Chico printed, "God's Wee Mate". They also used a permanent pen marker to write "God's Pal" on the side of my football boots and "Rev" on the underside. So I certainly did not need a dog-collar to identify me as the club chaplain. Besides, John had already explained my role very clearly to the players in his own inimitable way!

I thoroughly enjoyed training with the players. Running round the park, taking part in training drills involving passing and shooting – it was just brilliant. That was until John thought I could make the numbers up by playing in a seven-a-side game. Too far, Gaffer! You could tell by the look on the players' faces that they did not like this idea one tiny bit – especially if it meant I was playing for their team. I was usually last pick in the school playground when I was a kid, so you can imagine how the selection process played out in this instance. The two captains both dreaded having me in their team.

On one occasion, I had a particularly poor game. I had a great chance to redeem myself by scoring but I missed an absolute sitter. On 10 other similar occasions I would simply have tapped the ball into the net but, this time, in my eagerness to burst the net, I took a swipe at the ball and completely missed. All of my teammates were furious with me because they ultimately lost the game and who could blame them? Players are *always* competitive, even at training. The following week, I remember arriving at Firhill and I was not feeling too great about myself. I sat in the car praying, "Oh Lord, please help me not to mess up in training today, give me some supernatural skill so that the players will not get frustrated with me!" This was not a prayer that would be answered. I was reminded that I was not there as a player but as a chaplain and that I should get over myself and get on with the job of doing my best to help the players with everything in their lives *off the pitch*.

That day, the two captains made their team selections and, of course, I was last pick as usual. However, the captain who was going to be left with me asked the manager if he could be a man down rather than have me playing for them. When asked for an explanation, he replied, "Because he's ****, Gaffer. Even he knows that!" Keeps you humble! And good job I do not hold grudges. That player eventually became the manager – Alan Archibald. Mercifully, to all concerned, including me, Archie never involved me in the training at all when I was chaplain under him.

On one occasion, I went into John's office and said, "Gaffer, I really do appreciate you involving me as much as you do at training, but I think playing me in a bounce game is a step too far. The lads are getting frustrated with me. John replied, "Look son, I like the boys to relax on a Friday morning and they always have a good laugh at you falling on your **** - that's why you I give you a game, don't ever think it's because you're a player!" Cheers, Gaffer!

Personally I think that John Lambie should have been on the Queen's honours list – if only for managing Chic Charnley! If there is one player who could have done with having a full-time chaplain solely assigned to him during his career, it would be my good friend, Chic. He was a tremendously talented player but he had a short fuse, which perhaps explains why he was sent off more times than anyone else in the history of Scottish football – 17 times to be precise – over a career lasting 19 years.

John was the only manager who ever knew how to handle him and bring the best out of him. Chic tells the story of when he had been out socialising – in truth, getting very drunk – one Saturday night after a game. It continued longer than he had intended. In fact, he did not make it to training on the following Monday, Tuesday or Wednesday. His concerned manager decided to pay him a "pastoral visit" and told him that if he did not come to the training ground the following day, he would tell Chic's wife a few things that Chic might not want her to know! It seemed to do the trick, but by then the press were running a story about Chic's drinking exploits. John held a press conference and castigated the journalists for falsely accusing his player of being out on a drinking spree when the poor lad had been suffering with the man flu for nearly a week. He told them that Chic had actually dragged himself out of his sickbed to train on the Thursday, knowing there was such an important game that weekend. So, shame on you journalists! They believed John's story. Chic played that Saturday, scoring one and setting up another. His manager had stood by him in his hour of need – he was still fined £100 though.

Chic is perhaps best known for his altercation with a potentially deadly assailant during a training session in the 1990s. At that time, Thistle trained at public grounds in Ruchill Park, near Firhill. Today it is a beautiful green space affording great views across Glasgow but back then you would have been better advised to use your eyes to look out for any danger around you – it was not the safest place in the city. At one particular training session, they were accosted by a man wielding a samurai sword! Not perturbed by this potential threat, Chic picked up a traffic cone and *he* chased the would-be assailant and proceeded to attack him. A cut to his hand from the samurai-wielding thug was the only injury Chic suffered thankfully.

I got to know Chic when John Lambie brought him back for a very brief spell as a player and then to help with coaching. He is the sort of person that I would been friends with at school, and frequently ended up in trouble with. On one occasion, Chic and I went into the manager's office for a chat with him and, for a laugh, we decided to count how many times he swore in the course of a conversation with us. After a few minutes we burst into a fit of the giggles as we had both lost count. When he asked us what we were laughing at, we told him and he ordered us to **** off out of his office.

As a coach, Chic would show the boys how it was done during shooting practice, especially when it came to free kicks. He was still a technical genius. I usually joined in with the players at these times but it's fair to say that Chic was less than impressed when it came to my scoring prowess. If I had carried out his instructions to "**** off back to your

30

pulpit" every time I missed the target, I would never have been out of the church. I wanted to show him that I was good at other sports, so I took him on at badminton – he destroyed me. At least Chic only narrowly defeated me at table tennis, which is probably the sport at which I most excel. He is just one of these annoying people who is good at every sport!

Chic was not the only former Thistle legend John Lambie brought in to help with coaching. Alan Rough came in for a brief spell and I for one was delighted. For me, Roughie is one of the greatest ever Scotland goalkeepers, and he also played a starring role in Thistle's 4-1 defeat of Celtic in the 1971 League Cup Final – I don't think I have mentioned that game yet have I? I remember playing in a bounce game with Roughie in the opposition goal and I must have had three or four decent strikes on target. He pulled off one great save after another, showing that he still had it. Although let's be honest, it would have been embarrassing to allow the Rev to put one past you.

This brings me to my next story, my one glorious training moment which is worthy of sharing – mostly because it was about the *only* glorious moment! It was on the full length park. The ball was crossed in and Mark McNally headed the ball down right to my feet – what the heck was he thinking? 30 yards out, I caught it on the half volley with my left foot and it screamed into the top right corner of the net. I cannot remember who the goalkeeper was that day. I was recently reminiscing about my superb strike with Kenny Arthur, who was the first-choice goalkeeper at that time. He is adamant that it was not him in goal. He said that had it been him between the sticks, he would never have been able to look at himself in the mirror again! Whoever the goalkeeper was, I will still be telling this story to my grandkids, though by then, the strike will probably have been from 40 yards out.

The one position I have never aspired to play in is that of goalkeeper. On only one occasion was I asked to play in goals during a bounce game. I was terrified at the prospect and I had every reason to be. I expected no mercy nor was I shown any. If anything I am sure the shots were coming in harder than ever, none more so than by our midfielder, Paul MacDonald. He could not have been more than five yards away from me when he volleyed in a cracker, driving through the ball with his laces with every bit of power he could muster. Even though I remained behind the ball, my attempt to save it was in vain, as the ball *and I* landed in the back of the net while my glasses flew off in the other direction. Normally a goal is celebrated but on this occasion all the players fell about laughing instead.

After training on a Friday, the boys would vote on which player had been the worst performer that morning. The following week they had to bring in a supply of cream cakes for the squad – this was clearly before the days of sport dieticians. They were very gracious to me as I only ever had to bring them in once! On one particular occasion, as I sat in the dressing room enjoying my cream doughnut, Andy Walker, formerly of Celtic and Bolton, looked at my "ripped" upper torso and commented, "Hey Rev, I bet that's not *your* first cream cake sir!" To be fair, it did inspire me to lose a stone in weight after that.

CONFESSIONS OF A FOOTBALL CHAPLAIN

When John retired from managing Thistle in 2002, the club held a dinner in his honour. I was asked to say grace and offer a prayer of thanksgiving for John before we ate. To be honest, I am not used to saying this kind of prayer. I tend to talk to God as you would in any relationship, very informally and unscripted, but I was happy to oblige for the Gaffer. This was my prayer of thanksgiving:

Lord, we're here to cheer John's great career
Though men have robbed him of wealth
Giving thanks for success, we'd ask you to bless
And keep him in the best of health

Lord we give you praise that in recent days
He has begun to mellow
But he still gets mad if we're playing bad,
For he bleeds red and yellow

We pray he'll be here for many years
Before You blow the final whistle
And we'll always be grateful, that John's been so faithful
In all he's done for the Thistle

His love for his doos, makes all the news
But despite all his patter
We know it's Mamie his wife, the love of his life
His girls and grandweans that really matter

So bless John this day, look after him we pray

And save him from doing anything risky

Keep him in his prime, may he have a great time,

And help him go easy on the whisky!

Everybody at Partick Thistle acknowledges what an incredible job John Lambie did at Firhill. When he came back for his third spell in March 1999, the club had suffered successive relegations and were in danger of going down to the old Third Division, now League Two, the bottom tier of the SPFL. He made a wise move in bringing in his former number two, Gerry Collins. However, despite that and his previous successes at the club, John initially struggled to steady the ship. I remember early on in his third tenure, there were a lot of rumblings about whether he "still had it". Thistle only escaped relegation by a solitary point that season and the team won only two of their first 18 competitive games under him. In October 2000, John was facing the once unthinkable possibility of "losing" the Thistle support. But for his previous successful stints at Thistle, and the goodwill and hope they generated, I doubt he would have survived.

I will never forget the game that was the turning point. We were away to Queens Park at Hampden and won 1-0, thanks to a Danny Lennon goal. That slender victory ensured that John kept his job, and he not only survived, he thrived, and guided the club to successive promotions and a place in the top division.

Interestingly, on the weekend of that victory we held a special football outreach service at my church in Kilsyth. John and some of the players had expressed an interest in coming to my church at some point so I thought this would be a good opportunity to invite them, since our speaker at the service was my good friend John Boyers, chaplain to Manchester United. I even asked Mr Lambie to do the Bible Reading and say a few words to the church. Something, which if I am honest, I was a wee bit nervous about! I could just imagine him not being able to find the particular Bible verses he was to read and saying something like, "Och I cannae find these ****** verses…" I need not have worried, as mentioned before, John knew how to behave in the appropriate setting and he was brilliant. He later confessed to me that he had been more nervous about speaking in front of our packed church than he ever had been speaking in front of the television cameras or to a group of fans.

Not only did he do a sterling job with the Bible reading, he remarked on that fact that since John Boyers had become chaplain at Watford and then Manchester United, both clubs had gone on to enjoy great success. So why had this not happened at Partick Thistle? From the platform, he suggested that he was going to try and bring in John Boyers from United and give me a free transfer – the church thought this was hilarious! Having said that, John once remarked that he thought him coming to the church and bringing some of the players that weekend was a factor in Thistle's fortunes dramatically improving. But let's not go there, we saw what happened to Tommy Bryce…

I remained in touch with John after he retired. He had made it clear that he was not finished with using my services. He had one last job for me to do for him. He told me that he wanted me to conduct his funeral when "his time came". I was honoured to be asked but I hoped it would not be for many years to come. Thankfully, despite a number of health problems caused by keeping doos (pigeons), John continued to live for much longer than some people probably thought he would.

John remained a lifelong friend of the Club Doctor, Alan Robertson, who continued to help look after John's health. Alan recommended certain supplements. One of them, which he introduced to me and John, was astaxanthin – it sounds like a Greek party island doesn't it? Every time I visited John at his house he would introduce me to some other new health-promoting wonder. One supplement that he recommended, which I still take to this day, is organic turmeric. John swore by it! I mean, he swore all the time I know, but you know what I'm trying to say. Both astaxanthin and turmeric have an abundance of antioxidants that build up the immunity system and fight inflammation. I don't care whether it's a placebo effect or not – over the years that I have taken them and Vitamin C, I have not had the man flu and I have remained in excellent health, so that is good enough for me!

On one of my visits to John it was clear, that despite all his recent years of self-care, his passing away was imminent. He wanted to talk to me in a more detailed manner about what he wanted his funeral to look like. To quote him, "Now I don't want one of they boring, serious funerals, I want one of they upmarket ones…" I assumed he meant "upbeat!" I was left in no doubt about what he expected – not dour hymns but lively gospel music. I will tell you how that funeral went in the chapter, "We don't do death, Rev".

I certainly miss him – the phone calls and visits. My biggest challenge was when I took him out for lunch. He always tried to insist on paying so I would have to pretend to go to the toilet and sneakily foot the bill when he was not looking. John was such a kind-hearted man. In fact, one of my treasured possessions is my Partick Thistle kilt, which John gifted to me. I often wear it when conducting players' weddings. I was reluctant to accept such a gift from him but he convinced me to do so, "I'm too ******* skinny to get intae that now, you'll get more use of it!" Straight talking John Lambie!

Partick Thistle owe John Lambie a huge debt and so do I because he took a chance on this rookie chaplain. I would often remind him that if it was not for him buying in to chaplaincy the way he did, Sports Chaplaincy Scotland would probably not exist today. I hope I had a positive influence on him too. In his last spell at Thistle he was on a spiritual journey. He avidly watched the American Bible teacher and evangelist, Joyce Meyer, on the God Channel, and used to rave about her teaching on "positivity". So, for his 60th birthday, I bought him a book she wrote entitled, "Me and My Big Mouth". It's about how much more productive we can be in a leadership role when we use words that build people up rather than tear them down. No one flourishes under disparaging, denigrating and demeaning rants – everyone flourishes under encouragement and affirmation. Players who had been with John in his previous spells said to me that they felt he had mellowed with old age. But I think he had discovered the efficacy of positive psychology long before it became the norm.

CHAPTER 3

OTHER GAFFERS

John Lambie retired as manager of Partick Thistle in June 2003, taking up a seat on the club's board as an associate director. Gerry Collins, his assistant, took on the role as first team manager. I was delighted because I had built up a great relationship with Gerry and I was very hopeful that he would continue on from where John left off. Sadly, things did not work out for Gerry and he was sacked just five months later.

For me, one of the most challenging aspects of being a chaplain is watching a manager face the impending axe. You want to encourage them and speak positively about the challenges they are facing but you know how ruthless and brutal the professional game can be. Anyone going into management these days knows what they are letting themselves in for. For them, there are only three certainties in life – taxes, death and the sack.

When Gerry was relieved of his duties, John Lambie briefly returned to the hot seat in a caretaker capacity in December 2004, before Gerry Britton and Derek Whyte were appointed as joint managers. Again, I was delighted with their appointment because Gerry and Derek had been players with the club and I had a great relationship with them. It was always going to be a challenging transition moving from the dressing room to the manager's office but the players loved them and there was a great atmosphere around the place with them. However, it is a results business and just over a year later, on 19 December 2004, we were

39

playing Hamilton Accies at Firhill and the writing was on the wall. Word was that if we were defeated, Gerry and Derek were going to be sacked. The players did not want the management team to lose their jobs, they certainly had not lost the dressing room. However, we were defeated 1-0. After that game, I will never forget sitting in the Aitken Suite at Firhill with some of the players' wives and also Gerry Britton's wife. Everyone was so deflated and anxious. The axe was about to fall. There was nothing that could be said to make the situation better. This was the last Saturday before Christmas – not a great present for your kids to have to tell them you have lost your job. What the fans do not see, and in some cases, do not seem to care about, is the effect that facing the sack can have on managers and also on their wives and families. Thankfully for Gerry, after another couple of forays into management, he went on to oversee Thistle's Weir Youth Academy. He is currently the chief executive of Partick Thistle, doing a fantastic job – definitely the right fit for him. Why do I say that? As well as being an excellent footballer, Gerry studied Law at university during his playing days, and went on to qualify as a criminal defence lawyer. I remember him studying on the team bus as we travelled to and from away games, while the rest of the players bantered together. When you combine his experience as a player, coach and manager with his qualification as a lawyer, you can see why being CEO is a great fit for Gerry and the club.

The management team of Gerry and Derek was replaced with Dick Campbell, Jimmy Bone coming in as his assistant. Dick was a promotion specialist and Jimmy was a Thistle legend, scoring the fourth goal in our famous League Cup final victory over Celtic in 1971. Have I already mentioned that? I thought they were a great pair and they did what was asked of them by taking Thistle back up to the second tier, the First Division, now the Championship, via an epic play-off final against Peterhead.

We had lost the first leg of the final at Firhill 2-1. I never took part in team talks, but the following Friday after a training session, for some reason Dick asked me if I had anything to say to the players ahead of the second leg on the Sunday. This is not something that chaplains would generally do, and I would even go as far as to say, I would discourage it. I never want our role to be associated with performances or results. However, Dick asked, so I pointed out that I had noticed that after their first leg victory, the Peterhead players had celebrated as if they had already been promoted. If I had been a Thistle player that would have really wound me up and I said I hoped it would have the same effect on them. The important thing was to keep going right to the very end.

Five minutes into the second leg, Peterhead scored, which meant Thistle were 3-1 down on aggregate now. Thankfully, the Jags battled their way back into the game and just three minutes later, Mark Roberts brought them back into the game with an equaliser. We were still 3-2 down over the two legs, and that scenario remained two minutes into injury time. Keep going until the end! They did, and a Billy Gibson 25 yard free kick ricocheted off a Peterhead defender and into the net to spark wild celebrations among the sizeable travelling support. No goals were scored by either side in extra time so it came down to penalties, which

41

Thistle went on to win. We were promoted! Again, I take absolutely *no* credit for anything Dick, Jimmy and the players achieved. I had a church event on that day so I was not able to go to Peterhead for the game but I made my way down to Firhill at midnight to greet the victorious players as they came off, well in most cases, fell out of, the bus.

Despite achieving what was asked of him, the fans never really took to Dick. Some managers' wives attend the games, although I do not know why – I would certainly dissuade them, and Dick's wife often attended. The following season, I was sitting next to her in the Main Stand when a group of supporters in the Jackie Husband Stand, opposite us, unfurled a banner that simply read, "**** off Campbell". She was understandably very upset. At that time, I did something that I would strongly dissuade chaplains from doing – I got involved with the politics of the football club. Chaplains should keep their opinions to themselves, whether that is about how the team is playing or decisions that the board takes. We are there to support everyone, regardless of what is happening. However, I wrote in the club programme of my horror at the way Dick and Jimmy were being treated by some of the fans and I urged the board to back the management team.

In March 2007, Dick was shown the door at Firhill. Jimmy took over as caretaker manager until the end of the season, with Terry Butcher coming in to help him. What a big gentleman Terry was and he makes a fine cup of tea too! He insisted on making me a cuppa every week after training.

As I said, I was really saddened at how badly I felt Dick was treated at Thistle. He went on to manage Ross County the following season but was also sacked by them on 2 October 2007, only a few months into the job. Chaplains often stay in touch with managers and staff long after they leave the club and I had been no different with Dick. I phoned him up to try and give him some words of encouragement and comfort because I really felt for him. I need not have worried. Dick has had so many knocks in the game that he is very philosophical about everything. He said to me, "Dinnae worry about me Mark son, I'm getting paid up by both Thistle and Ross County and I'm relaxing in my garden and enjoying the odd game of golf. And I'll tell you something else – Dick Campbell will be back!" True to his word, he went on to manage Forfar Athletic and he was there for seven years. At one stage of his stint there, he was the longest current serving manager in Scottish football. Of course, the inevitable happened there too when he was sacked after a string of bad results, but I know that this was the most difficult decision the club chairman had ever had to make.

It is worth mentioning that I know most club chairmen in Scotland and I do not believe any of them have ever relished sacking a manager. Off the top of my head, I can think of three chairmen who have opened up and told me of how sacking their manager left them feeling utterly distraught. They had grown close to the manager and had appreciated all he had done for the club, especially if he had brought success. Thankfully, Dick bounced back as usual, and at the time of writing, he is enjoying an incredibly successful spell as manager of Arbroath.

Back to Partick Thistle. The following season, after Dick was sacked, Thistle appointed Ian McCall as manager. I was looking forward to working with him. I came down to Firhill during the close season to meet with Ian and all seemed to be good. However, I got a call the following week from him to ask me to come back down to see him at the club. He delivered the most devastating news I could have imagined. He said he had been told to tell me that the club no longer required my services! I was absolutely shell-shocked. Nine years I had given to the club free of charge and they were letting me go, just like that? I could not understand what I had done wrong. The decision made no sense. And what was worse – nobody at the club was accepting responsibility for the decision to sack me. Ian said it was the board's decision, whereas someone on the board insisted it was Ian's decision. Regardless of whose decision it was, it actually turned out for the best. Not only for me but also for the development of chaplaincy in Scottish football.

One of my favourite verses in the Bible is Romans 8:28: "And we know that in all things God works for the good of those who love him, who have been called according to his purpose."

This simply means that, because of the personal relationship I have with God, no matter what happens to me, God will use it for a good purpose in my life. I have proved this to be true time and time again. So whoever made the decision to show me the Firhill back door, I forgive you and thank you at the same time because things turned out fantastically well!

It was at this time that the Scottish FA had started to invite me down to the UEFA A Licence coaching course in Largs, to deliver a seminar outlining the basics and benefits of chaplaincy. The time that I had previously given to Thistle, I was now able to dedicate to speaking to other clubs about chaplaincy – even though I didn't think I was a very good advert for a chaplain, given that I had just been sacked as one! Over the following four years, the number of club chaplains grew from a small handful to 22 of the SPFL clubs – more than half.

In April 2011, Ian McCall left Thistle and stayed away from management for about four years before taking on the role at Ayr United. Thankfully, he was able to keep their chaplain, who had nothing but good things to say about him. Since then Ian has returned to Firhill and the current Thistle chaplain thinks the world of him. It just was not meant to be for me to work with him but I am glad he has had the benefit of the service of other chaplains.

Things have consistently changed at Firhill over the years. By April 2011, there was a new board and a new manager. Jackie MacNamara took over the reins and, while I didn't know Jackie at the time, I knew his assistant Simon Donnelly, who had previously been signed as a player by Dick Campbell. I asked Simon if Jackie would be open to a conversation about chaplaincy and he arranged for me to meet him. I walked into his office and Kenny Crichton, the physiotherapist at the time, was also present. I did not even get a chance to explain the role of a chaplain before Kenny said, "Chaplaincy's a great thing Gaffer. When I was at Gretna, their chaplain was a great support to me when my dad died..." And that was that! Kenny is one of my favourite people within the game. He has many of the qualities of a chaplain – a really caring person with a great listening ear. Jackie invited me to return as chaplain and it sounded like a dream come true. Back at my beloved Firhill! And yet within me I did not have a peace about returning to Thistle at that time. This was confirmed by one of our chaplains, Neil Urquhart, who said that he thought it would be better if I placed someone else in at Thistle. I could then continue to use my day and a half a week to develop the work of chaplaincy in Scottish football. I had really missed the dressing room banter and was so excited about getting back into the swing of things but I knew Neil was right. So, with Jackie's permission, I started looking out for a new chaplain. Thankfully, I found a top man in Craig Denham but it did feel like handing over my child for adoption!

In less than two years, 30 January 2013, to be precise, more change was afoot at Firhill. Jackie MacNamara and Simon Donnelly were lured away to Dundee United, which meant that Alan Archibald, still a player at the club, was thrown in at the deep end as the new manager. He brought in Scott Patterson, his former teammate, as his assistant. When Jackie and Simon left for Tannadice, there was a lot of concern around Firhill that Thistle's push for promotion to the Premiership would be derailed. Would the team become unsettled? Archie was considered by many to be too young and inexperienced to take over the reins. However, his and Scott's record turned out to be even better than that of their predecessors. Thistle went on to deservedly win the Championship, gaining promotion to the Premiership – and the Jags played some of the best football I can ever remember. As a chaplain, you have to walk through some dark times if the club is in trouble, but it also means you get to share in the good times. I must admit, I looked on with a bit of envy as I saw Craig sharing the joy of the players. I could remember what that was like. But at the same time I was so delighted with the fantastic job he was doing there. In those two years that Craig took over, I continued to speak to other clubs and the number of chaplains in the SPFL grew from 22 to 36.

At the end of his second season, Craig dropped a bombshell by saying that he was going to have to lay aside the chaplaincy for an indefinite period, because of additional church responsibilities. At first I was really disappointed, but my wife, Aileen, said she felt that it was right for me to go back to Firhill for a while. It had been six years since I had worked at the coal face. If I was to give relevant ongoing training and support to chaplains, it was important for me to know what issues people within the game were facing now compared to the past. What great wisdom this proved for me – as it usually does with Aileen.

As mentioned elsewhere, I was now working two days a week with Sports Chaplaincy Scotland, so it meant I could work for Thistle but still oversee the rest of the chaplains. Another positive was that I had known Archie since he had been an 18 year old player, making his way into the first team. I had also known Scott as a player too. One of the things I admired about the management team was that they genuinely cared about their players. They wanted the best for them and seemed to be able to bring the best out of them. They did not berate or humiliate the players, recognising that such a style of management is very unproductive. Their man-management skills were superb and that was one of the reasons why they were so successful. Of course, they had their ups and downs, their good and bad runs of results, but from my perspective, they always appeared to remain calm under pressure and that spread through the dressing room. It also helped that they had a good relationship with the board and with Ian Maxwell, the managing director, now CEO of the Scottish FA.

This may sound strange, but one of the most cherished memories I have of my second spell at Thistle was when they were having a poor run of results. Some fans were typically calling for Archie's head but the chairman at the time, David Beattie, issued a statement that went something like this: "Regardless of how this season ends I can categorically say that Alan Archibald will still be our manager next season." I was never so proud to be associated with this club. And the effect? Within a couple of games we were back on track and ended up finishing the season very strongly, without any danger of relegation. At one stage Archie was the second longest serving manager in the SPFL after Jim McInally at Peterhead. He eventually met the fate of nearly all managers, although I know it was the most difficult decision the board at that time had ever had to make.

There are few more fickle and fragile industries. When you hear that a manager has signed a "three year contract" you begin to wonder what that actually means. If someone is given a contract then it should be honoured by both sides - end of! Certainly, there can be clauses within that contract that allow a bit of leverage on both sides. For example, it could be agreed that if the team is languishing in a certain position at a particular stage of the season, then the club has the right to sack the manager at that point.

I remember congratulating a friend who was a manager of an SPFL club, just after he had won a trophy. Many others had been praising his accomplishment too. However, he said, "Mark, when people are patting you on the back, they're just feeling for where they'll stick the knife in later!" Sounds very cynical, doesn't it? Well, he was proved to be right as he was sacked less than a year later.

As I will explain in the chapter, "For if you know the history...", I went on to become chaplain for the Scottish FA, so I had to relinquish my role at Thistle after one and a half seasons of being back. I handed the baton back to Craig, he eventually passed it on to Andy Brady, who was much loved by everyone at Firhill, before Jonathan De Groot came in and he is still doing a sterling job at the time of writing.

For me, management is the hardest job in football. You are under pressure from so many different people – chairmen and directors, players and fans. It's certainly not a job you could depend on to pay your mortgage. You have to be thick-skinned, because fans can attack you in so many ways now. It's not just banners being unfurled in stadiums, or protests outside the gates. The worst form is on social media.

I suppose I sympathise with managers even more than players because I had a stint at management myself, albeit with an amateur club. Before you go searching for me on Wikipedia, let me start by saying it was a team that played in the Strathclyde Evangelical Churches League. However, if you think I was dealing with a bunch of sweet choir boys then think again!

During the same period that I was appointed as chaplain to Thistle, I became the senior pastor at Kilsyth Community Church. This led to me being the chaplain to fifth and sixth year pupils at Kilsyth Academy. I became aware of some talented young local footballers in those year groups who did not have a club to play for. They were often aimlessly hanging around drinking Buckfast ("Buckie" for short) tonic wine throughout the weekend. I wanted to give these boys something more productive to do with their time so I decided to start KCC FC. I had the wisdom to immediately hand the running of the team over to two enthusiastic individuals in the church, Gordon and Stewart. I took on the role of chaplain, same as at Thistle. They had their ups and downs but did a great job. Eventually Stewart moved to Dundee and Gordon became a dad so his priorities understandably changed. It looked like the club might have to fold so I heard myself offering to take on the role of manager! Now, bear in mind this was amateur football. I was not under any pressure from anyone to succeed and there was no one to sack me because it was my team, but I took it so seriously that results probably affected me more than I would care to admit.

The transition from chaplain to manager was a lot harder than I could have imagined. You are effectively having to say, "Jesus loves you as a person, but as a player I think you're mince and I'm dropping you!" No more Mr Nice Guy! My first two games in charge ended in heavy defeats and I was furious. I warned the boys that unless there were significant improvements I would be releasing players and bringing in others. We won our next game 11-1 but, instead of encouraging the players afterwards, I went into the dressing room and yelled, "See! That's what we're capable of! So never think I'll tolerate a performance like what you delivered in the first two games". I did learn to become more of an encourager!

I empathise with managers who clearly instruct their players on what is expected of them positionally and tactically and then watch in frustration as if nothing has been taken on board. It just takes one player to miss an easy chance or another to lose concentration and instead of scoring you can concede within seconds – such incredibly thin lines between success and failure. I think it's very important for a manager to play to their strengths and learn to delegate to others who are strong in areas in which they are weak. I was a good man-manager and motivator but my coaching skills were non-existent. Not that I was so aware of these failings myself. That was until after a game, when a couple of players suggested that I try and bring someone in who was a proper football coach!

I tried to think of someone I knew who was local, who in football terms, was currently at a loose end. Oh, and someone who would be willing to come and work with me for free. Easy – George Shaw! George had become a good friend during his last spell as a player at Partick Thistle. He lived in Cumbernauld and had recently been sacked as manager of Forfar Athletic, so I knew that he was currently out of the game. I decided to phone George one Friday night. The timing of my phone call could not have been more perfect. At the moment I phoned him, he was "out of the game" but in another way! Former Thistle player, Ray Farningham, was one of George's best friends and had invited him to his son's wedding. Let's just say that when I spoke to George that Friday night he was in "high spirits". He answered his phone, perhaps not able to speak as articulately as he normally would, "Awright wee man how's it goin'? I cannae hear you too well, what are you saying about it…." I said, "George I need a favour. I'm managing this football team but we need some top class coaching to take us to the next level [George loves it when you massage his ego]. Any chance you could take pre-season training and then if you feel you've got something to work with, could you come in as first team coach?" "Sure, wee man, anythin for my wee pal. Nae bother!" I wasn't too sure if he had actually taken on board what I had asked him. Sure enough, the next day his wife said to him, "George, do you remember your phone call with wee Mark last night?" He had no recollection. "Well", she said, "You've agreed to get involved coaching his team, so you'd better do it!" George is a man of his word. Not only did he take pre-season training, he put the boots back on and became player-coach. Even in his 40s, he was man of the match in most games – different class. No one could match his ability, his work-rate –

or his tan! The only challenge I had with him was trying to stop him arguing with referees. I am sure I was not the first manager to have that problem with him though. It was an ideal partnership – a good cop/bad cop sort of arrangement. I eventually handed all responsibility over to him for training and team selection. A great move, as we enjoyed promotion to the top flight in our leagues. After four years, with the growth of chaplaincy, I was no longer able to continue with the football team but I am glad I had the experience because it give me a little insight into the pressures managers are under.

On one occasion, I brought John Lambie along to a game and asked him to give the half-time team talk. It was 0-0 at that stage and I had been disappointed with my team's motivation levels. I said, "Gaffer, give them both barrels, don't spare them, give them a rocket." Honestly, if you had heard him you would have thought he was talking to his grandchildren! He was so kind and gentle in how he spoke to them. Afterwards, George Shaw said, "Gaffer how come you never used to speak to me like that?" John replied, "Cos you were a ****** professional and should have ******* known better – these guys are amateurs." We won 4-0!

Even though it was me who changed things around in the second half, switching from a 4-4-2 formation to 3-5-2 so that we could exploit the space down each flank and get decent balls into the box, from which we scored all of our goals, John was convinced that our victory was all down to his inspirational half-time team talk – and who was I to argue?

CHAPTER 4

WELCOME TO GLASGOW!

One of the roles of a chaplain is to help new players settle in, especially if they are from foreign soil. They can find the culture just as difficult to adjust to as the style of play. At Partick Thistle, we had our fair share of players who came from afar, so as a chaplain, I was able to help with the challenges of homesickness and loneliness. My wife is an absolutely brilliant cook – she can turn her hand to many international cuisines and she often does so to make foreign guests feel at home. On the other hand, I am absolutely brilliant at inviting people for dinner *before* asking Aileen if it's okay for them to come. Hosting the players in our home took them out of the dressing room environment and enabled them to relax and be themselves. That really helped me in terms of getting to know them as a person, not simply as a player.

Quinton Jacobs, a Namibian internationalist, came to Partick Thistle via Germany. He simply could not get to grips with the dressing room. He could not understand why everyone seemed to hate each other and why the other players were so unkind in the way they spoke to him. I had to sit him down one day and explain to him the concept of Glaswegian humour. "Quinton, welcome to Glasgow. See if the lads are really horrible to you, it's because they accept you and if they say nasty things to you it's because they like you…" He just shook his head and said, "This place is crazy!" He was not wrong to be fair.

I do have a particularly funny memory involving Quinton. I occasionally drove him to his digs in Bishopbriggs after training as this was on the way to my home in Kilsyth. One night I said to him that I would have go home via the city centre as I wanted to look at a French restaurant on King Street. I had heard good reports about it, but I wanted to check it out before booking a table there for my wife and another couple. I struggled to find it because of a temporary one-way system, so I stopped the car in the Saltmarket. This was in the days before phones had mobile data so I could not "google" the eating place. So, I called my wife to find out the phone number of the restaurant so I could ask them for directions. As I was speaking to Aileen, I heard a knock on the passenger window. "Hold on Aileen", I said, "I think someone is stopping to give us directions." Quinton pressed the button to wind down the window. "I'm looking for King Street please", I said, as it dawned on me that I was actually talking to a rather scantily clad woman. "Oh right boys, are you not looking for business then?" My wife was still on the phone at this time and thankfully found it hilarious that we had been accosted by this prostitute. "Er, no, King Street will do fine thanks!" I replied. She did give us directions and off we went. Quinton turned to me and asked, "Did you know her Rev?" "No, Quinton, that was a lady of the night, you know, a prostitute. I can categorically assure you that I have never met her before!" I am not sure he was convinced.

This is one of those scenarios that you rarely get to keep quiet. That Friday morning, I was called into the manager's office. John Lambie was loving this! "I'm thinking of making a bit of money, giving the Scottish

Sun a story about a minister leading a Partick Thistle player astray by taking him into the red-light district!" I would not have put it past the old buzzard!

A few years later I was on the "Off the Ball" radio programme with Stuart Cosgrove and Tam Cowan and I made the mistake of sharing this story with one of the programme researchers prior to us going on air. It would not have been like Tam to miss an opportunity like this, so I should not have been surprised when he started to ask me about rumours circulating that I had been kerb-crawling in the Saltmarket! Such was the red colour of my face I was glad it was radio and not TV. As an aside, for me "Off the Ball" is one of the best things about Scottish football. I tune in every Saturday on my way to and from the match I'm attending. It never fails to be entertaining. Before Tam took on the radio show, he had a successful TV series called "Offside." I'm surprised it ever got off the ground because I was one of his guests in the pilot series. I was on with Colin McCredie, former star of the TV series Taggart, and an avid St Johnstone fan. Even though Tam was his usual hilarious self, mostly at the expense of me and the Jags, there was not a budget for a live television audience at the time so it was down to just me and Colin to laugh at Tam's jokes. I did not want to look like a stereotypical minister, so I dressed in white jeans and a bright purple shirt. I can assure you it was in fashion at the time – I just can't remember on what planet it was fashionable. I suppose that, in itself, was asking for a slagging and maybe just one of the reasons why Tam only had me on his radio show thereafter. If you look up "Offside" on Wikipedia, it says that the programme began with "only minor footballing guests, however in its later times more widely known celebrities appeared, such as... Kevin Keegan." Aye, you're welcome Kevin, happy to have been a warm-up act for you pal!

Back to showing Quinton around Glasgow... To be fair, I did take him to more reputable areas of the city than the Saltmarket. His favourite was the Botanic Gardens, near Maryhill. There was one section that hosted a number of Namibian plants and he was so animated to see that which reminded him of home. As we walked through the gardens, I could not help but notice that he said "Hello" to just about every black person he saw. I was intrigued, so I asked him if he knew these people. "No" he said, "It's just a black thing!" Certainly, at that time Glasgow had many people of Asian ethnicity, but not so many of African or Caribbean descent, so it actually makes sense. I have been going out to Rwanda just about every year since 2008. In some areas white people are very rare – the locals stare at you as if you are from outer space and you do find yourself saying hello to someone if they are of the same skin colour for that reason alone. On occasion, we would invite Quinton to our house for dinner and we invited other African friends to try and make him feel at home. He seemed to really appreciate that.

Thistle signed a goalkeeper, Jakup Mikkelson, who had to leave his wife and three children behind in the Faroe Islands, in order for him to pursue his career in Scotland. Jakup was used to living in wide open spaces back home, but now he found himself living in a tiny hotel room in Kirkintilloch. Jakup needed to get out, so, as well as offering him hospitality, I took him and another player, Jean Yves Anis, a Frenchman, hillwalking in the Campsie Hills, near Glasgow. Not only was this good for their fitness levels, it also did their mental health the world of good. Gerry Britton was the co-manager with Derek Whyte at the time, so I made sure I had their permission to take the players – Gerry even wrote an article about our expedition in the Herald.

I love telling people of the time we signed a player from Liverpool FC – Scott Patterson. I felt there was some poetic justice in this because Liverpool has taken the great Alan Hansen from Firhill for a paltry £100,000 back in 1977. Scott was so comfortable on the ball, an expert at converting defence to attack within seconds. His swashbuckling style and calm attitude actually reminded me of Hansen. Scott is Scottish but he had married a local girl when he was with the Reds. When Thistle signed him, his wife dutifully followed him with their little daughter. Many people do not appreciate how difficult it is for a player's family to be continually uprooted as they move from club to club. Scott's wife found it very difficult living in Glasgow, cut off from her family in Liverpool. She did not know anyone in Scotland and, understandably, it was upsetting for her. As a consequence, Scott was feeling guilty that he had dragged his wife away from her family. I asked what she had done for a living and he told me she was a beauty therapist. So, I suggested that my wife put on a supper night and Scott's wife could offer to provide some beauty therapy for the other players' wives and girlfriends. There was a great response, just about all of the players' partners were up for it. All I had to do now was inform my wife that she was going to have a house full of WAGS! Thankfully, she was as gracious and welcoming as ever. The players' partners came to our house, enjoyed the food, wine and beauty therapy. But most important, that night friendships were formed that continue to the present day. Scott's wife, Jo, was happy, so he was happy and Thistle felt the benefit. The fact that the family has continued to live in Scotland to this day demonstrates that it's not such a bad place to live as long as you have good friends.

The upshot of that situation was that Thistle gave me permission to open the "Family Room". On match days, I looked after all the wives, girlfriends and parents of players. It was an aspect of my role as chaplain that I absolutely loved and it definitely made a positive difference to the experience of players' families. When we signed a player, part of my personal introduction to him included offering to meet his family at the front door of the stadium on the day of his first game. I would take them to the Family Room and introduce them to the rest of the families. Billy Dodds had a brief spell with us at the end of his career. Billy is a man of many clubs but he said to me that he could not recall being anywhere where his family had been made to feel so welcome.

The Family Room was also very useful in gaining an understanding of the pastoral issues with which the players were struggling. In fact, most of the pastoral situations I found myself supporting players in were actually instigated by their family members, whose trust I had gained. Increasingly, players would ask their wives, girlfriends or parents to have a word with me in order to explain their situation - rather than directly approaching me after training. Being with the players when they were with their families helped me to get know them so much better because they no longer felt the need to "perform" and try and portray a certain image as they often did in the dressing room.

I had the joy of conducting many players' weddings. I used to find it hilarious that when they were in the dressing room they would talk very freely, openly and explicitly about sex. However, when I brought up the subject of sex in pre-marital counselling, they were somewhat embarrassed when broaching the subject in that scenario!

Initially, we were able to show excellent hospitality to the families at Firhill, but as cost-cutting measures had to be taken over the years, it was reduced to custard creams and rich tea biscuits. While I would never dismiss these traditional favourites, I felt it did not give the right impression to families of professional players. There was only one thing for it – I bought in some decent biscuits myself each week. When the families realised I was having to do this, everyone started to chip in. Some people even brought tray bakes and home-made cakes. The standard was excellent.

I have heard that the club has considerably upped their game since Jacqui Low became chairman – apparently they are even served pies at half-time! This does not surprise me, Jacqui deeply and genuinely cares for everyone connected with the club. She recognises that it is just as important to value players' families as it is to value the players themselves.

During Dick Campbell's time, he was keen to sign a big Finnish player, Jukka Santala, on loan from Rangers. There was also a Dutch club interested in him, but Dick wanted to demonstrate to the player that Firhill would be the best choice for him. Jukka had a Glaswegian girlfriend, so Dick invited them to a game, giving me instructions to look after them well. I don't know how much their visit to the Family Room influenced Jukka's decision, but his girlfriend was certainly very keen for him to sign for us after her experience. We signed him as a defender and initially things did not go well for the big man – so much so that some supporters began to wish he had moved to the Netherlands after all. However, in one particular game Dick was short of options up front and decided to play him as a striker, since he was such a tall lad. Boy did he start to deliver, he became a goal machine! Having a Scottish girlfriend certainly helped big Jukka settle in. However, often a player has to move to a club with a partner who is also from a different culture.

One such case was the big Belgian defender Frederic Frans. I immediately took to Fre – he was such a pleasant guy. He had recently married Valerie and so she came to Glasgow with him. Initially, they had to stay in various hotels but there were so many difficulties with their accommodation that it caused them a great deal of stress. Aileen and I helped them move into their own apartment and we would invite them for dinner. I took them for drives in the car to some beauty spots nearby, giving them space to go off for a romantic walk together by a loch. My favourite memory is when I took them to Stronachlachar by Loch Katrine. It did them so much good to get away from the busy city and it also helped them appreciate what an incredibly beautiful country Scotland is. Valerie was very similar in nature to my youngest daughter and I treated her as if she was one of my own offspring – she called me her Glasgow dad. They have since moved back to Belgium but we keep in touch. As a chaplain, you can form relationships that supersede football careers.

It is worth pointing out that sometimes Thistle signed a foreign player and it simply did not work out for them. Imagine having the challenge of being in a strange culture, compounded by the frustration of not getting the opportunity to play. One example of this was a young player who we signed from the famous FC Barcelona – Simon Colina Dominguez, to give him his full name. He was a terrific young player with amazing technical ability. However, he was used to tiki-taka (or tiqui-taca, to give it the correct spelling). This is a Spanish style of play, characterised by short passing and movement, working the ball through various channels, and maintaining possession. The style is primarily associated with the club Simon had previously been at, Barcelona, especially during the era of Pep Guardiola. Simon was slightly built, and his style of play perhaps was not best suited to the more physical Scottish game, so he never played for the first team. His attitude was first class though and I always felt that if he did not get his breakthrough in Scotland it would happen somewhere else. He was a delight to host in our home – so mannerly and grateful for anything you did for him. My wife and I would have happily adopted him! Currently, he is playing in the Norwegian First Division and I am really glad things worked out for him. The vast majority of young players will be released by a club at some stage in their careers but it's important to remember that when you are let go it's only someone's opinion! Sometimes you need to persevere until you find the right club with the right manager at the right time for you.

Perhaps the most exotically-named player we signed at Thistle was the Mexican, Gabriel Rojo de la Vega – or plain Gabi as we referred to him. He came to us from Rayo Vallecano, the Partick Thistle of Madrid. The reason I say that is that they too were overshadowed by two much larger and noisier neighbours – in their case, Real and Atletico. Maybe that was part of the attraction for Gabi to come to Firhill? I always felt with Gabi that if football did not work out for him, he could have a career in modelling. He was an incredibly handsome guy. My wife maintains that Gabi was not her type – she obviously prefers wee, baldy, specky, beardy, scrawny types like me. All I am saying is that when Gabi came for dinner, she always made sure he was sitting opposite her… Mind you, this meant that I was sitting opposite his stunning Spanish girlfriend, now his wife, Carlota, so I was not complaining. Chilli con carne never tasted so good! I took them on one of my Scottish countryside tours in the car. Despite the scenery being undeniably beautiful, unfortunately, all the winding roads caused Carlota to get rather travel sick. It did not turn out to be the romantic jaunt I had planned for them. Ultimately, it did not work out for Gabi at Firhill, so he and Carlota moved back to Mexico. Gabi did not become a model as I would have predicted, but he eventually started a very profitable fitness coaching business. That they were both very fit is certainly undeniable!

When we have dinner together as a family, we always make a point of giving thanks to God before we eat – saying "grace". However, when we have guests for dinner, we do not like to embarrass them by imposing our values and practices. We simply tell them to get started as we inwardly give thanks to God for his provision. However, that did backfire on us one time. We had invited a couple of French players for dinner, the aforementioned Jean Yves Anis, and our striker, Armand One. I said, "Just get stuck in lads!" Big Armand looked at me in shock and disappointment and said, "Are we not going to give thanks for the food first?" "Sorry big man, sorry – you're quite right", I said, as I sheepishly bowed my head and prayed.

CHAPTER 5

THE AGONY OF INJURY

Partick Thistle won the Second Division, now League One, in 2000. The following season, they went on to win the First Division, now the Championship. They had secured back to back promotions leading us back to the Promised Land – the Premier League. They were playing St Mirren at their Love Street ground on the day they won the First Division, winning the game 2-0 to clinch the title. As Derek Fleming scored the second and decisive goal, the St Mirren goalkeeper challenged him and Derek's tibia and fibula were broken. A double leg break – horrific. That night, the Thistle players were back at Firhill having a right old knees up. Me? I was in the Royal Alexandra Hospital in Paisley with Derek, as he was coming to terms with what could have been a career-ending injury. This is an example of what chaplains are there for – to support those for whom "living the dream" of becoming a professional footballer, has become a nightmare.

In that game against St Mirren, Scott McLean suffered a foot injury. While his injury was not as serious as Derek's, it still required medical attention. I had left Scott in the waiting room of the accident and emergency department, while I was with Derek. However, it was clear that perhaps it was not the best place to leave Scott. It was a Saturday night, he was in his Partick Thistle tracksuit, and we had just defeated the local team. There were a number of Saints fans in the A&E department who were rather inebriated – and they were giving Scott pelters. Feeling it would be safer to take him elsewhere, I offered to

65

drive Scott to Hairmyres Hospital in East Kilbride instead, as it was near where he lived. Scott asked if we could drop by Firhill on the way there so he could "get something". When he got out of the car he refused to get back in. He said he would rather stay for the celebrations with the boys and see to his foot in the morning. There then ensued a stand-off – well actually a sit-off. I was sitting in my car and Scott was sitting on the pavement – determined he was not going to go to any hospital when he could be celebrating with the boys! I knew John Lambie would go off his head at Scott if he limped into Firhill. He would also lambast me for not taking him to hospital as I had promised. I must have spent half an hour arguing with him, while he sat on the pavement in the huff with me because I would not help him get in to the party. Thankfully, he eventually saw sense. Either that or he realised that the celebration would not have been much fun, given the rollicking he would have received from the manager. I was exhausted when I finally got home that night, some celebration for me!

Serious injury is no laughing matter though. It is probably the biggest concern of any player – apart from falling out of favour with the manager or a new manager coming in who does not like you. When a player has a bad injury, it is not just him who is affected – his loved ones can become very anxious. Here is an example, which thankfully has a good ending. Partick Thistle were playing Ross County on the last day of the season 2013/14. Neither team needed to win to stay in the Premiership, but there was enough at stake to make it a very competitive match. The further up the table the club finished, the greater the prize money, so there was quite a lot riding on this game financially. In what appeared to be a fairly innocuous situation, our goalkeeper, Scott Fox, rose to confidently catch a crossed ball. However, the Staggies' centre forward challenged him and, although he failed to win the ball, he landed on top of Foxy's ankle. It looked like a horrendous injury – a bad break for sure. A horrible silence descended on the crowd as Foxy lay in shock and agony. He was stretchered off. Meanwhile, I was sitting in the stand with the players' families as I normally did. His fiancée Charlotte was behind me, deeply worried and close to tears. I went to the physiotherapist's room to find out how serious the injury was. Foxy was going to be taken to the hospital and an ambulance was on its way. I came back up to the stand to inform Charlotte of what was happening and offered to take her to the Western General Hospital as, by this stage, she was too upset to drive. As we followed the ambulance, Charlotte tearfully told me that at the end of the season she and Foxy had planned a holiday in Florida. She had really been looking forward to Disneyworld – she is a *big* fan of all things Disney – but if Foxy had a broken ankle, there was no way they would be able to enjoy their dream holiday. Always wanting to bring a positive perspective to these situations, and with a dash of inappropriate humour, I said, "Well, look on the bright side, Charlotte, if Foxy's done his ankle he'll be in a wheelchair and you might get to the front of the queues for all the rides…" Thankfully for me she was able to see the funny side! Foxy's injury did not turn out to be as bad as was first feared and they were able to go on their holiday. I also had the pleasure of conducting their wedding two years later.

By this stage, ironically, Foxy had moved to Ross County, the club whose player had accidentally caused the injury that we feared may finish his career. He faced a lot of "banter" from Thistle fans when they played County – you can imagine some of the names he was called. When conducting the wedding rehearsal, I was so tempted to jokingly say, "Do you Scott Peter *Judas Iscariot* Fox take Charlotte… to be thy lawful wedded wife?…" Of course, I would never have done that. On their wedding day, Charlotte was every bit the beautiful princess she is and Foxy was doing what he normally did to balls being crossed into the 18 yard box – he was punching! As a footnote, Foxy eventually saw sense and came back to Firhill as a Thistle player.

In 1999, Thistle had a promising 24 year old player, Alan Morgan. Premiership clubs from England were rumoured to be watching him. His future looked so bright. I will never forget the incident that led to Alan's horrific injury as long as I live, partly because it looked so innocuous. Thistle were playing against East Fife. Alan and an opponent were going for the same ball. The East Fife player slid in and Alan jumped over him. There was no contact but Alan landed awkwardly. It did not seem serious, yet Alan ruptured both the cruciate and lateral ligaments in his knee. However, the worst part was that he also damaged a nerve which ran down his leg and that left him with what is called a dropped foot. Even then, we were all sure he would be back after a period of convalescence. However, after 10 months of attempted rehabilitation, Alan was given the devastating news – there was no hope of him playing again. At one stage, the specialists considered a nerve graft, but decided this would not be the answer. Everyone at Firhill was in shock. It just seemed so unfair. I cannot imagine how Alan must have felt but through this devastating time my wife and I became good friends with him and his fiancée, Lynsey. I had the pleasure of conducting their wedding blessing the following year.

As a humorous aside, I have to confess that I was late for the service, which was obviously Lynsey's prerogative. Now, in my defence, it was in the days before sat-nav and it was in Livingston. This "new town" has around 800 roundabouts, I am reliably informed, so if you take just one wrong exit you are scuppered! Alan was standing at the front of the big hotel conservatory, waiting for his bride to come down the aisle, but something did not seem right to him. Something was missing, or more to the point some*one* was missing – the minister! He had to call down to the ushers to tell Lynsey to hold back because I was not there yet. When Aileen and I finally arrived, about half an hour late, it's fair to say that our relationship had become fairly fractious by this stage. There was a lot of mutual blame being exchanged for taking that wrong exit about 15 roundabouts ago! Imagine the scene – all the guests are in the conservatory watching Aileen and I walking up to the hotel having a right rammy – in plain English, "a robust altercation". Of course, when we walked into the service we had to put on that smile that said, "We *never* have arguments…" Our friends know us better! We all managed to have a great laugh about what had happened and the wedding blessing turned into a great celebration. Alan went on to complete his A Licence coaching course and now works with the Scottish FA. It would have been so easy for Alan to walk away from football, but it has been great to see him have such a positive impact on so many other aspiring players.

Another player whose career was cut short through injury was David McCallum, who Thistle signed from Motherwell. He was one of the best corner and free kick specialists I have seen, and a great passer of the ball. However, he had a bad knee injury while at Thistle. We grew close, as I took him for treatment at the Nuffield Hospital on a regular basis. The specialists tried their best to fix David's knee, but ultimately it was in vain. He eventually left Firhill to play part-time at Queen's Park, but finally retired at the age of only 27. Does that sound like a bit of a downward spiral? David did not allow it to be so. A month after he retired, the Spiders offered him the role of Under 17's coach, and less than 10 years later, he was overseeing one of the most successful youth development squads in Scotland. This group of players included Andy Robertson, who, at the time of writing, has just won the English Premiership with Liverpool and will likely have a crucial role in upcoming international matches for Scotland. I am sure Andy would list David as one of a number of important influences throughout his career. David obtained his A Licence and Pro Licence badges and went on to work for the Scottish FA as Coach Coordinator. Then he took on the roles of Technical Coordinator and Assistant Development Team Coach at Rangers. It would have been so easy for David to have walked away from football. The disappointments he experienced could have made him bitter or better, in his case, his afflictions certainly made him better. I actually feel like the McCallum family chaplain. David married his childhood sweetheart Mari and I had the pleasure of taking part in their wedding service in Luss, by Loch Lomond. Much as it was a beautiful day and a wonderful occasion, my lasting memory of it was the midges getting right up my kilt and causing severe problems, especially while all the photos were being taken. In the years that followed, I had the pleasure of conducting a blessing service for each of their two daughters. And, sadly, I conducted the funeral of David's brother too. But that is what a chaplain is for. They are there to help you celebrate the good times but also to support you through the dark times.

It is bad enough when a player suffers an injury in a game or at training, but what about the impact of a horrific injury outside of football? Willie Howie came through our youth set-up at Thistle. John Lambie gave him his first team debut at the age of 16 in May 1999 against Queen of the South. He was tipped for a big future. However, in 2001, Willie was seriously assaulted near his home, leaving him with a fractured skull. He spent a month in hospital. Initially, we feared for his life. Then there was a concern that he would have permanent brain damage. It was certainly very doubtful as to whether he would play again. It was at that time, with Willie still gravely ill, that John Lambie gave him a new two year contract. That tells you all you need to know about John. He had no guarantees that Willie would ever play again, but he wanted to make sure that the lad and his family would be okay. I am quite sure that John would have done anything else necessary to ensure Willie and his family did not suffer any more than they already had. As a chaplain, I walked through that horrendous time with Willie, regularly visiting him and trying to encourage him. Thankfully, he did recover, and returned to the Thistle first team in November 2003 for a game against Aberdeen.

Back to the impact of serious injuries on players. I feel this is something that many supporters do not fully appreciate. If a player suffers an injury, the question usually is, "Have you got someone else who can take the shirt?" But try for a moment and put yourself in a player's position who appears to be seriously injured. For people in some professions, an injury may signal a temporary setback and a short time of recuperation but for professional footballers the implications may be far-reaching. When a player initially realises that his injury is severe, he is likely to be filled with fear, worrying about how long he will be incapacitated. To him, each day is like an eternal moment, it can seem like there is no end in sight. Watching your teammates from the stand and seeing them celebrate a victory can create so many mixed feelings. The injured player can feel so disassociated from the success. They may possibly think, will I ever be back in the manager's plans? Will I get another contract? Will I ever play again? Will I be the same player? The mental torment can actually be worse than the physical discomfort and pain.

And it's not just on match days – it can be very lonely and demoralising for a player when he watches his teammates go to the training ground while he remains alone in the gym or with the physiotherapist in rehabilitation. It is those players that the chaplain is particularly interested in getting alongside, offering words of hope, encouragement, and, if appropriate, prayer.

I have also known players who thought that their injury was due to divine retribution or abandonment – I would like to think that our very presence and compassion acts as evidence that God is, in fact, deeply interested and concerned for the injured player.

CHAPTER 6
THERE'S A GHOST IN MY HOUSE –
AND OTHER SPIRITUAL STORIES

I have told the next story at many secular events as well as churches. I have found that it has sometimes made even the hardest cynic become more open to spiritual realities. I received a phone call one Thursday night at around 11:30pm from my good friend Scott McLean, our star striker. Here's how it went:

"Rev, I'm really scared, I need your help. I haven't been able to sleep properly for the last three months. Every time I'm drifting off to sleep I feel like something's on top of me and choking me!"

Not taking him that seriously to begin with, after all, he was the joker in the dressing room, I jested, "Are you sure that's not your missus trying to strangle you mate?"

"No Rev, I'm serious! And it's not just that. The dog is going mental, barking at one of our bedroom walls for no reason at all. And we can't get our room to heat up, even when the radiator is on full blast and is roasting to touch. There's no draught coming in the window but our room is always cold and damp even when the rest of the house is okay. And there's just a horrible feeling in the house, I think there's something spooky going on!"

I wasn't too sure what to make of it. I had been involved in delivering homes and people of demonic influences in the past. What I normally do in such a situation is try and explain away what is happening naturally

74

and, if that doesn't work, I consider that I may have a supernatural situation to deal with. I continued the conversation:

"Okay, I'm happy to have a look, when do you want me to come down?"

"Right now Rev, right now!!"

"Mate, it's nearly midnight and we've got training tomorrow morning!"

"I know Rev, but now that I've told you about this I'm really terrified and there's no way I'm going to sleep a wink tonight – please come now!"

I drove half an hour to his home. As soon as I entered the house, I could tell that there was a bad spiritual atmosphere, particularly in the room Scott had referred to. It turned out that one of his neighbours indulged in occultist practices and had come round to his house and cursed him, for no apparent reason. That's his version of events anyway!

I was not sure what he was expecting me to do but I explained that my method of deliverance was quite simple and needed no props. Now, I do accept that some of you reading this will think I am talking absolute nonsense, but stick with me, read what happened and then, by all means, make your judgement.

I explained to Scott that as far as spiritual power is concerned, for me, Jesus Christ is the top man. After rising again from the dead he ascended to heaven. Today, he reigns over every other spiritual power – and that includes Satan, who in terms of spiritual authority, is under Jesus' feet. Now, because I am a follower of Jesus, I share his authority over Satan and every demonic power. They have more reason to be afraid of me than I do of them! So, I explained that I would simply command any demonic entity to leave the room and tell them to go to wherever Jesus would send them.

I know this must sound hard to believe but this is what happened next. There was a tangible manifestation and something like wind swept past us and left the room. Still cynical? From that night, the dog never barked at the wall. Still cynical? From that night, the room was comfortably warm, the heating worked perfectly. Still cynical? Well, let's go to the next morning.

I had said to Scott that it might be wise for him not to tell the rest of the players about what had happened as they would probably slaughter him. Remember, his nickname was Trigger for good reason! The next morning, I was sitting in the dressing room. It was only five minutes before we were due to leave for training at 10am, and any player who arrived late was fined. There was no sign of Scott. I was slightly concerned. Suddenly, the dressing room door flew open and in he marched. As he did so, he shouted across the dressing room, in full hearing of the rest, "Aw Rev, thanks for what you did for me in my flat last night mate. It was brilliant! That was the first decent night's sleep I've had in three months!"

I sat there horrified. That statement was going to require a fair amount of explaining. It did not sound good on so many levels! Some of the boys started to snigger. One of the players beside me could not hold back and asked, "Trigger, what was the Rev doing in your flat last night and what did he do to give you a good night's sleep?"

It got worse. Scott responded, "Aw it was brilliant boys, the Rev got rid of all these ghosts!" That is *not* how I would have explained the situation, not at all! At this, the players simply fell about laughing. At one point, Scott Patterson went off to the cleaning cupboard and came back with "Henry" the cylindrical vacuum cleaner – and began to sing, "Who you gonna call? Ghostbusters!"

In the midst of all this hilarity, John Lambie walked in. Now, this was a Friday morning. They were meant to be preparing for a big game the following day and all he could see was absolute mayhem as players were keeled over laughing. "What's going on?" he demanded. One of the boys piped up, "Aw Gaffer, you'll love this, the Rev has been in Trigger's house last night and he got rid of all his ghosts!" John laughed and replied, "Ach, I don't believe that at all! Even ghosts wouldn't be stupid enough to go into Trigger's house!" Cue, more hilarity. That was pretty much the flavour of the entire morning and over lunch time. However, after lunch was finished, one of the players came up to me privately and said, "Erm, Rev, I've been having funny goings on in my house, can you come and sort me out too...."

Sure enough, various things were falling off the shelves in his bathroom for no apparent reason. At first, I wondered if it may be due to vibrations caused by lorries driving by his house, but then I discovered he lived in a very quiet cul-de-sac. When I went into his bathroom, I tried everything to get items to fall off the shelves. Jumping up and down, banging the walls, everything I could think of to naturally explain what was happening. I was stumped. There was only one explanation left to me – a supernatural one. So, I prayed, commanding anything not of God to leave that room and the house. From that day nothing ever fell off the shelves in this player's bathroom. Go figure!

After training one Friday, a player approached me privately and said, "Rev, I'm really struggling with an asthma type problem. I'm having to get taken off after an hour because I can hardly breathe. The doc can't work out what's wrong with me and he's putting it down to some mysterious virus. No one seems to be able to get to the bottom of it. Can you pray for me?" Now, at first I wondered if he was taking the mickey, because that was what Mark Roberts normally did! However, I could see he was in genuine distress so I said, "Of course, I'll pray for you, but I could also pray *with* you if you want?" "What's the difference?" Mark asked. "Well" I said, "If I pray for you I'll be doing that at a distance, but if I pray *with* you, I'd be laying my hands on your chest. Sometimes it helps increase faith and connection with God." "No chance Rev, absolutely no chance! I've seen that God Channel on the TV. People got hands laid on them and they were flying across a stage, mental stuff! No chance, not for me Rev. Besides, God would probably strike me down if you did that with me after all the slagging I give you!" While I thought this was hilarious, I agreed that I would just pray *for* him!

The next day my wife and I were travelling down to the game in our car and Mark phoned me. "Rev!" he rasped, "I need you to pray for me, this is serious mate, I can hardly breathe!" "Of course", I replied, "But remember the offer is still there to pray *with* you!" "No way Rev – just pray *for* me!"

I arrived at Firhill, and as soon I entered through the Players Entrance door, Mark grabbed me and said desperately, "Rev, pray *with* me!" The only place in the stadium where I thought we would have any privacy was the tiny boot room, so off we went. I explained what I was about to do, that it was just a simple and straightforward prayer, and we would wait and see what God would do. Imagine the scene. We are in this tiny boot room. Mark is sitting on a stool. I have my hands on his chest and I am praying for him. And in walks the "tea-girl", Fiona! Try explaining that one to her. Thankfully, I knew Fiona very well. In fact, to merely call her the "tea-girl" is disparaging because she has been such a key person at the club over many years, faithfully serving in many ways, beyond making a very fine cup of tea for the manager and the referees. Back to the story. Fiona had been along to my church, as I had conducted her wedding, so the scenario was not too strange to her. Mind you, I am still trying to work out why she even came into the boot room...

Anyway, Mark played a full 90 minutes and over the forthcoming weeks he performed without hindrance. Yet, he never mentioned the situation during the rest of his time at Thistle. I used to wonder if I had actually imagined or exaggerated what had happened. Years later, he became the manager of Ayr United. When I went to visit him, he brought me into his office and in front of all his coaching staff announced, "Boys, God healed me of this chest problem when the Rev prayed with me years ago!" Yes, that's right, when I prayed *with* him!

These situations are not common – they happened over 18 years of chaplaincy work. At least it's good to know that if there is a problem at a football club, that defies a natural explanation, you don't need to call Ghostbusters. The chaplain may well have the tools to sort it for you!

Chaplains are pastorally proactive and spiritually reactive. This means that we are proactive in terms of supporting mental and emotional needs but reactive in terms of addressing spiritual needs. We will not instigate discussions on spiritual matters, nor will we impose our beliefs, however, we will respond to spiritual requests and questions. We are always happy to give spiritual help, advice and guidance when asked. What we cannot do is pray that a player develops a better first touch or that he will score a goal! You get the picture...

As I said, we do not initiate discussions of a spiritual nature but there have been times when I have offered to pray for someone, or indeed *with* them, and I have invariably found that even if the person has no faith in God, they have gratefully accepted my offer. On some occasions, the person perhaps did not want to receive prayer, but they were very appreciative of the gesture as they recognised it was a sign that they were genuinely cared for.

There have been quite a number of well-known Christian footballers playing in Scotland over the years. Marvin Andrews, Stuart Elliot and Brian Irvine became friends of mine. It was interesting to get their perspective on the challenges of wanting to live a Christian life in a very secular environment. At Thistle, we signed a Christian player on loan, George Moncur. George's dad, John Moncur, had been a famous West Ham United player, a real hard man of the ilk of the late Norman ("bites yer legs") Hunter. John had autographed quite a few opponent's shin-pads in his time himself. He was also well-known for being a heavy drinking, bad tempered character. When he became a Christian, his teammates could not believe it, and they gave him the ribbing you would expect. It's fair to say he did not become a "softie". He was still a hard tackler, though not as dirty as before. His life was completely transformed for the better and his family noticed. George was one of three sons and he, along with his brothers, was so impressed with the change in his dad's life that he made his own decision to follow Jesus. You have heard of people wearing their heart on their sleeve? George had this big tattoo on the upper part of his right arm that said, "I can do all things through Christ who strengthens me", a quote from the Bible. He was not shy about telling the dressing room that he loved the Lord and he even asked the manager at the time, Alan Archibald, if I could pray with him before games. Archie was fine with that, as long as it did not interfere with his team talks.

I have always found it a bit of a challenge knowing what to ask for when praying for players. As I have mentioned, we do not pray for divine favour, success or victory. Christian players are not exempt from injury or disappointment and I do not believe that God favours them in a sporting context. I believe that when Christian footballers pray, they should ask God to help them give 100% of themselves in wholehearted commitment to their manager and teammates and that they will not cheat their opponents in any way or cause injury to them. I do not see self-centred requests to score or win as a legitimate use of prayer.

CHAPTER 7

MAGALUF MAYHEM!

Towards the end of season 2000/01, in which we had won a second successive promotion, Danny Lennon, the club captain, said to me, "Rev, we want to thank you for everything you've done for us this season, so we're going to take you on holiday with us!" This was typical of Danny – always trying to include me in anything that was going on. I really appreciated him. "Where are we going Danny?" "Magaluf", was the reply. Yes, indeed, they were going to take me to Spain's finest cultural tourist destination...

To be honest, I was naïve. I thought that we would play five-a-side football in the mornings. I also took my tennis racket with me, thinking that some of the boys would give me a game in a sport in which I could actually compete with them. In the afternoon, I assumed that we would relax by the pool, and afterwards, we would enjoy a pleasant evening meal together. Then I thought we would all retire to bed, glad of the opportunity of an early night, after the rigours of a long and exhausting season... Naïve does not even cover it. Magaluf = Carnage.

A common tradition with footballers going on holiday together is for everyone to dress the same or similarly. The dress code for Magaluf was to be the most gaudy, flowery shirts we could find. From the moment we arrived at Glasgow Airport, all of us looking rather conspicuous, most of the party started drinking. Some of them did not stop until we got home. Someone in his wisdom thought it would be a good idea to book us into a quiet family hotel – at least, it was a quiet family hotel until we arrived.

Humour in a football dressing room can be best described as "inappropriate". However, such jocularity does not really translate in a family hotel setting. One of the group who had been on the lash since we had been at Glasgow Airport walked past two middle-aged bikini-clad ladies who were rather on the heavy side. He offered the following observation, "Ladies, that cellulite looks beautiful on you two!" They were not impressed. He was not meaning to offend anyone but his banter with other residents of the hotel was not being well received and I was getting really concerned that someone would write to the club to complain. I thought, "There's only one thing for it – I need to get this player sober! I need to tell him what he has been saying and doing and get him to apologise to all the offended parties." With his permission, I locked him in his room and took all his money, banning him from going out. It did the trick, he sobered up – the next day I took him to all the people he had offended. To be fair, he was horrified at himself, as he would never have offended anyone intentionally. Job done! However, as soon as he was allowed out it was not long before he was causing mayhem again, albeit he did not offend anyone. After the trip, this particular played suggested to John Lambie that he sign me as a defender because I had been the best man-marker he had ever come across!

The evenings were eye-openers for me. In fact, we should really have called them "very late night/mornings" because the lads were going out when I would normally be going to my bed. Indeed, on the first night,

I opted to not go out with them, instead I wisely retired to bed early. In the morning, after breakfast, I picked up my tennis racket and tried to find someone to have a game with, but the only players I met were those who were just arriving back from their night out. Clearly I was going to have to adapt to their new time schedule if I was going to see them. If you can't beat them, join them!

At the beginning of the night, the group would be together but gradually it would dissipate as some players began to go their own way. At that stage of proceedings, I decided that it would be safest to hang around with our goalkeeper, Kenny Arthur. He had become a good friend and we used to play squash together back in Scotland. I don't want to humiliate Kenny by telling you who usually won but all I will say is – don't entertain his accusations that I cheated – I am a chaplain after all! Kenny was also studying at university for a degree in Risk Management at the time. He was one of only two players in the squad who were preparing for life outside football in this way. I have already mentioned that Gerry Britton was studying Law. Anyway, I considered Kenny to be the most sensible and responsible of the Magaluf group.

On reflection, the choice of Kenny for company was a good one. We had a great time socialising with others, while remaining unscathed by the mayhem around us. My only concern was that I would be able to stay awake. Kenny offered a solution. "Try this Rev, this'll keep you going for the night…" He handed me a can of Red Bull. Even though the energy drink had been launched in 1987, I had not even heard of it at that time, far less sampled it. I downed most of a can of this caffeine-laden drink before going into a night club. I did not have time to finish it so I thought it would be okay to take it in with me. The bouncer disagreed. So I said, "Okay, well can I put it on that window ledge, and will you look after it for me until we leave pal?" The look on his face suggested that he could tell I was not a frequent visitor to this kind of establishment. The advert for Red Bull says that it "gives you wings." Well, it seemed to give me a new pair of feet! I was cutting moves on the dance floor that would have made John Travolta look like a bad-dad dancer. I'm not saying I was moonwalking but I was definitely on some other planet. There is no doubt, this beverage kept me wide awake all night, but it continued to do so for the next three nights.

To be fair, there was another reason why I found sleeping a big challenge – my roommate, Michael Max, who was the only other non-player on tour. He was the stadium announcer but he has taken on many other roles over the years at Firhill. Now, Michael is a very pleasant guy who quietly goes about the business of serving Partick Thistle. But he is not quiet at night. When he snores he sounds like a wounded warthog. Now I knew why I was meant to bring my tennis racket! I placed it strategically by the side of my bed every night and as Michael inevitably woke me up with his snoring, I thumped him with my newly adapted weapon to shut him up. It actually did the trick momentarily, but I would have to repeat the action several times throughout the night. That was until Michael had enough of the beating and advised me that if I hit him again with my racket, he would insert the handle somewhere that would be very painful. There was only thing for it, stay on the Red Bull, stay up and stay out. As I have said, if you can't beat them, join them!

Even on the plane back home, some of the boys were behaving in a rather boisterous manner, one of them being Danny Lennon. He was trying to banter with *everyone* round about him, including the person seated directly behind him. He turned round and quipped, "Hey, are you talking behind my back?" He also tried to banter with the air hostess but she was having none of it. After several warnings, she asked the pilot to have a word with him. Up the pilot strode, very officiously introducing himself to Danny: "I am the captain of this plane!" Before he could continue, Danny replied, "Aw that's lovely, I'm the captain of Partick Thistle, Danny Lennon. Nice to meet you!"

On that return flight there were two less people than had embarked on the outgoing journey. We had a young lad with us, who only came on the trip because one of the senior players, Derek Fleming, had been seriously injured in our title-winning game against St Mirren. The lad was under 18, and really should not have been allowed to come with us, but what could possibly go wrong? On his first night out with the group he was downing peach schnapps and lemonade. That may sound innocuous – but he was a diabetic. The next morning he took seriously ill, and I received a phone call, asking me to come and see the player immediately, as some of the squad were very concerned. There he was, lying on the floor of his hotel room in a semi-conscious state. He was coughing up a black, tar-like substance. One player turned to me and said with absolute clarity, "Rev, I don't think he's very well!" Never say footballers lack intelligence! Having said that, another player, said, "Rev, I thought he was having a hypo so I gave him a Mars Bar!" Maybe not the best thing to give a diabetic who has just overdosed on sugar. We called for an ambulance. Thankfully the lad survived, but spent the rest of the week in intensive care. I visited him every day while the rest of the group slept off the excesses of the night before. The doctors reassured me that he would recover in time to be able to travel back to Glasgow with the squad at the end of the week. Because of these reassurances, I was under strict instructions from the players not to tell anyone back home about the lad's hospitalisation. It came under the "what happens in Magaluf, stays in Magaluf" rule. I complied with their ruling. Imagine my horror, then, when I went to collect him on the day before we were due to fly back home, only for the doctor to tell me that the lad had not sufficiently recovered in order to be released. The hospital was going to keep him in for observations for a few days, just to be on the safe side, so he would not be out in time for the homeward flight. I offered to stay on in Magaluf with him, but the lad's best friend in the team insisted that he would stay instead. That night, we frantically tried phoning the young player's mum and girlfriend to tell them not to come to Glasgow Airport the next day to pick him up but we could not reach them. When we landed on Scottish soil, it soon became clear to me why the lad's best friend had stayed with him and had not come back to face the boy's mother – she was a formidable woman! She was understandably angry and worried at the same time, though she did eventually get her son back safe and sound. To be honest, after our trip to Magaluf, I needed a holiday!

Despite the exhausting nature of the trip, I had thought it had been a lovely gesture for the players to take me to Magaluf with them. However, I later discovered one of the reasons I had been invited on the trip. A couple of players' wives/partners were not going to allow their men to go on the trip unless I went too, thinking that I would be a good influence on them – that worked well didn't it?

The following season, having been promoted to the Premier League, Partick Thistle continued their good form and comfortably avoided relegation. Time for another celebration – in Magaluf! I decided against going with the squad on this occasion – the previous year's trip was enough to last me a lifetime. On his return, Danny Lennon confessed that he wished I had been with them. Not so much because I missed a lot of fun but because he could have benefited from my "pastoral care".

That year, the players had decided that they would all dress in the same "uniform" for the holiday in Magaluf – tight, bright red tracksuits, as worn by the Russian national football team in the 1970s. To ensure that authentic tight look, they ordered tracksuits that were all one size smaller than what would normally fit them.

The players arrived at Palma Airport in good spirits. However, it seemed to be taking a long time for their luggage to be loaded on to the carousel. The belt was going round and round – with nothing on it. To alleviate his boredom, the captain and leader of the party, Danny Lennon, decided to sit on the carousel, followed by another three players – enthusiastically singing the old disco classic by the Gap Band, "Oops upside your head, say oops upside your head…"

Danny continued to lead the sing-song at the front of the chain of players as he passed through the flaps and found himself outside where they load the suitcases. What he did not realise was that the other members of the chain had jumped off the carousel before they too landed outside, so that he was now on his own, still cheerfully singing at full volume, "Oops upside your head, say oops upside your head…" Much to his chagrin, there were two Spanish police officers waiting on him – and they were not looking for his autograph! The officers casually lifted Danny off the belt and proceeded to severely castigate him. He was used to receiving a ticking off from John Lambie, so this was mild in comparison. They held him back while all the other players collected their luggage and departed for the bus to the hotel.

There was a further sting in the tail. Danny was the told by one of the officers that he would need to pay an "on the spot" fine of €200. If he did, they would release him with no further consequences. Danny felt that he had no choice but to take his punishment.

However, his challenges were not over. As you may know, alcohol is a diuretic and Danny had consumed plenty of it, prior to his arrival at the airport. Added to that, he had spent a considerable amount of time being detained by the police officers. To say that he was desperate to go to the toilet is an understatement.

Alas, he never made it in time and his tight, bright red "Russian 70s style" tracksuit trousers now had a very obvious wet patch, further adding to his embarrassment. Worse still, Danny could not find his luggage. Thankfully, one of the players had collected it for him and had taken it to the hotel for him. But there was yet another issue – Danny could not remember the name of the hotel where he and the players were due to stay. He had no way of contacting them because everyone had left their mobile phones in Scotland due to the roaming charges prevalent at that time.

Danny took a taxi into Magaluf and asked the driver to drop him off in the town centre. He sat outside Mulligan's Pub for two hours, while he searched the horizon for a large group of lookalike Russians from the 1970s. He was never so glad to see a bunch of bright red tracksuit-wearing individuals slowly but surely coming up over the hill.

He cannot remember much more of the next five days, but he did wish he had brought the Rev with him as his chaperone. As for the Rev, when Danny told me the story I was glad I stayed at home!

Danny was certainly not a heavy drinker as a player, he enjoyed celebrating at the end of a successful season, but that was the extent of his alcohol intake. After Danny retired from playing football, he obtained his Pro-Licence coaching badge and has become a well-respected, successful – and teetotal manager.

While I hope you have found this chapter funny, I feel it would be irresponsible of me to end it here. Let me ask you a question: who would you say were the best players that each of the Home Nations of the United Kingdom have produced? This is my opinion:

Scotland – Jim Baxter. Pele exclaimed that he wished Jim Baxter was Brazilian because he would have loved to play alongside him. If you mention Baxter's name to any Scotland supporter it is likely they will refer to the time when he tormented the England World Cup winning team at Wembley in 1967, helping the Scots to an easy victory.

Northern Ireland – George Best, who was an incredibly naturally gifted footballer. Best probably peaked in 1968, when at the age of 22, he had won three major honours in club football – the English First Division, the European Cup, and the European Player of the Year award.

England – Paul Gasgoigne. I have only seen television footage of Baxter and Best but I had the privilege of watching Gazza play when he was at Rangers. I remember a section of Thistle fans goading him throughout the game but he had the last laugh when he scored a sublime goal – what a talent!

Wales – Gareth Bale. He must be one of the best players in the world today, and a major reason why Wales surpassed everyone's expectations by reaching the semi-finals of Euro 2016.

Who is the odd one out? Gareth Bale. Why? He is the only one of these players whose career has not been adversely affected and brought to a premature end through alcohol abuse. And I don't believe that will happen either. Gareth has been teetotal since he was a child, when his parents gave him a drink one Christmas – he simply did not like the taste and that was that.

Nowadays, there is much more awareness of the harm that excessive alcohol can have, not only on sporting performance, but also on the physical and mental wellbeing of players. It is hard to think about Baxter, Best and Gasgoigne without wondering what they could have achieved had it not been for their relationship with alcohol.

I certainly do not want to come across as judgemental. As you will find out elsewhere in the book, I cannot say I have never been irresponsible with alcohol – far from it. I am not pointing the finger at anyone. But I do love to see people fulfil their potential, and it deeply saddens me when that does not happen due to poor lifestyle choices.

Further, I believe that the main determining factor behind the choices we make is who we allow to influence us. As I explain elsewhere, part of my role as chaplain to the Scottish FA was to work with the seven performance schools throughout the nation, which have been operating since 2012 to support the development of Scotland's best young footballing talent. Football coaching takes place during regular school hours within an appropriate timetable that compliments their academic studies and their club football team. The ethos is very much about producing well-rounded people as well as talented footballers.

One of the workshops I delivered was entitled, "Dealing with peer pressure". I used the following phrase throughout the workshop: "He who walks with the wise grows wise – and he hangs about with numpties becomes a numpty!" I gave examples of exceptionally talented players who "never made it", largely because the company they kept encouraged them to adopt a lifestyle that could potentially lead to a range of addictions. I also gave examples of talented players who *nearly* "never made it" but thankfully changed their friendship group just in time, before they prematurely dropped out of the game.

As an example of the power of peer pressure, I asked the group if any of them thought they were physically stronger than me. Naturally, having looked at my scrawny frame there was no shortage of challengers. I usually opted for whoever appeared to be the tallest and strongest. Then I set out the rules of the contest to decide who was the strongest. My challenger had to stand on top of a school desk, while I remained on the ground. He had to try and pull me up on to the desk, while my task was to pull him down to my level. The experiment demonstrated that it is easier for someone to drag you down to their level than it is for you to pull them up to yours. Of course, I invariably won and there were howls of protest at the unfairness of this competition. No illustration is perfect though, I must admit there were a couple of occasions when, despite my gravitational advantage, I was close to defeat! The main point is that they understood what I was trying to communicate to them – choose your friends carefully. Choose friends who want to help you be successful at everything in life, not just football. The positive mentoring of young footballers is crucial to their development and chaplains can play a vital role in this.

CHAPTER 8

WHAT ABOUT THESE CONFESSIONS?

I have listened to my fair share of confessions from footballers but I am not perfect either. So, there's no point in calling the book "Confessions of a Football Chaplain" if I don't share some with you! I will start with one that most married male football supporters can probably relate to but then I will give you three more that are unlikely to be what you would expect from a chaplain.

Back in season 1999/2000, Thistle were in the third tier of Scottish football and we were up against Livingston, who played in the second tier, in the fourth round of the Scottish Cup. Even though we were underdogs, I was really looking forward to the game. However, there was one major logistical challenge – I, my wife and young daughters were due to go on holiday, flying out to Gran Canaria from Glasgow Airport that evening. We had to be checked in at 5:30pm. There was no way I would have enough time to go to the game, drive back from Maryhill to Kilsyth, and then leave home for the airport.

The sensible person may well have concluded that attendance at the game was simply not possible that day. Far better to make sure all of the family arrive at the airport in good time and thereby guarantee a stress-free start to the holiday. Far better to start the holiday off on good terms with your wife. But since when did "sensible" belong in the vocabulary of a Jags follower?

I tried to explain to my wife that morning, "Aileen, the boys need me… I really think I should be there… You and the girls could get a lift to the airport from our friends… I could get a lift from one of the players after the game… Would that be okay?"

"You do what you want!" was the frosty reply from Aileen. Except I did not really pick up on the "frosty" bit – I took what she said literally. I wanted to go to the game and Aileen had said I should do what I want. So I went to the game. That sounds logical doesn't it? Seemed reasonable to me.

Going out of the door, just to check she was definitely okay with arrangements, I said, "So I'll see you at Glasgow airport then?" She replied, maybe even more frostily than the last time, "Fine!" So everything was fine then. Good.

Just to be doubly sure, because I really was picking up this frosty vibe by now, I asked, "Are you sure you're alright about this, is something the matter?" This time Aileen, said, slightly louder than in our previous exchanges, "Oh no, there's *nothing* the matter with me, just you go and enjoy yourself at the game and I'll deal with all the hassle of getting the girls and suitcases to the airport and just hope you get there on time!" The main part of her sentence I heard was, "Just you go and enjoy yourself…" So I did! What a great wife I have…

Of course I have learned a lot since then. The key thing is, *what* your wife says is almost irrelevant, it is *how* she say it that matters – sense the tone!

CONFESSIONS OF A FOOTBALL CHAPLAIN

Mind you, what a game it was that day. Tied at 1-1, Scott McLean came on and scored what proved to be the winner. A fantastic 2-1 victory – we were through to the quarter finals of the Scottish Cup! Even better, it was Scott and his brother Donnie who were taking me to the airport after the game. What a happy journey that was! When I arrived at the airport, *just* in time, I was deliriously joyful. Let's just say Aileen was not. She has the most beautiful green eyes – but they can be like laser beams if she is angry with you. The first few days of the holiday were rather difficult to navigate as she was still annoyed with me. Did she give me the silent treatment? I wish! I have had mates who have told me that their wife has not spoken to them in three days. I can only wonder what that must be like. At this point, I would like to say how sorry I am to Aileen for my thoughtless and selfish behaviour that day. I genuinely would *like* to say how sorry I am, but oh my, it was worth it....

To set the scene for the following stories, I need to explain a tension that exists for us as chaplains. We want to be one of the boys, but we know that we cannot be one of the sheep. In other words, we want to join in the banter and fun of a football club dressing room, while not speaking or behaving in such a way that might discredit us as chaplains. We do not want to come across as judgmental or *holier than thou*, but we recognise that our language and lifestyle will probably be a bit different to some people working in a football environment.

So having explained the context, here is how I made a complete mess of things during my time at Thistle! I realise that in telling these stories I run the risk of plummeting in some peoples' estimation of me. Others will just see the funny side of the stories and wonder what the fuss is all about. Either way, I assure you that anyone who knows me well will probably tell you they were out of character for me and I have also learned a lot from these mistakes.

Deep breath, here goes, let's start with arguably the first major bloomer! That same season of the Scottish Cup win over Livingston, Thistle went on to win the Second Division, now League One. On the day that the Jags were crowned champions, the celebrations were fantastic. What a great crowd gathered at Firhill that day. I stood at the side of the pitch, watching all the players assemble together in the middle of the park, ready to receive the trophy. The club doctor, Alan Robertson, grabbed my arm and led me on to the pitch to become part of the celebration photograph with the team. I felt a wee bit embarrassed but went along with it. I think that photo still hangs in the main entrance at Firhill to this day.

Afterwards, Danny Lennon brought me into the dressing room and I sipped champagne out of the trophy with the players. Then we went into the Aitken Suite for a buffet supper and we continued celebrations long into the night. Now, I enjoy a glass of red wine with a meal, but I would not consider myself a "social" drinker. However, that night I got caught up in the emotion of the occasion. I was not really taking stock of what or how much I was drinking, though I certainly didn't have the intention of over-indulging. My last clear memory from the night was standing at the bar talking to Peter Lindau, one of our players, and then suddenly the lights went out – and I don't mean the lights in the Aitken

Suite! I collapsed – I was out for the count. I vaguely remember the cool evening air hitting me as I was carried out of the stadium by George Shaw and his wife and into their car. I also remember wondering why on earth I had such a huge white napkin tied round my neck, to later discover it was actually one of the table cloths that I had already been sick on. George did not want me to vomit in his car as his wife was driving me home, so he thought I was as well taking the already-soiled table cloth home with me.

The next thing I vaguely remember is receiving a less than warm welcome from my wife when George dropped me off at my front door. I certainly don't think he took much time to say anything in my defence. He was off and left me to my rollicking in case he got into trouble for allowing me get into that state. He need not have worried. It was I alone who was responsible for getting into this sorry mess and Aileen typically did not leave me wondering if I had made a huge mistake! I was embarrassed and ashamed. Worse still, this was on the Saturday night and I had to preach the next morning at my church in Kilsyth. Believe me, I was in no fit state to do so. I remember that Sunday morning well. I was standing in the vestry shaking and sweating. I was also really worried that someone from Kilsyth would find out about the night before as this may well have led to a few people calling for me to be given my P45!

The town of Kilsyth has an unusual relationship with alcohol. People from the town had told me stories from during the coal mining era, when many miners would spend their meagre wages on alcohol at the end of the working week. This would result in terrible poverty and abuse in many families throughout the town. Kilsyth was consequently one of the last "dry" towns in Scotland – there was no licensed hotel until 1967. The local churches had generally taken a hard line against alcohol. Most of the local Christians were teetotal, due to the damage the over-consumption of alcohol had caused in the town historically. At that time, it would have been bad enough for some people to know I enjoyed the odd glass of wine. However, to discover I had been paralytic and then preached the following morning would have been too much for them to stomach.

From the perspective of being chaplain to Partick Thistle, however, here was I, the one supposed to be setting a good example to everyone, a model of moderation. Yet, I had been completely miroculous, and no, I didn't misspell miraculous! It was a "minor indiscretion", in the words of the chairman. It was a source of great hilarity for the manager and players. For me, I learned a huge lesson. I actually became teetotal for a year after that and I decided, thereafter, to take my car to players' nights out, knowing I would not be able to keep up with them in the drinking stakes!

Despite that personal misdemeanour, I have found club social events to be valuable opportunities to break the ice and build relationships with players. We signed a player who had never had any experience of a chaplain in any previous club, and I could sense that he was struggling to connect with me. His wife gave birth to twins and I had brought in a wee present for them, but he did not seem overly impressed with it. I just thought I would have to accept that some people at a club just won't engage with you. However, when I attended the players' night out, after he had a few pints, this particular player confidently came up to me and gave me a big hug. He said, "I think it's brilliant having a chaplain at the club. I've never had this before and it's a great idea and that was really kind of you bringing in a present for my kids, you're a top man Rev!" I was gobsmacked and I hoped he would remember this conversation when he was fully sober! Thankfully, he did and we became friends. That was when I discovered that sometimes it's not that players don't like you but they may not know how to relate to you as a chaplain, perhaps because they perceive you as a religious authority figure. That is why I always stress that the chaplaincy role is not primarily a religious one, but more of a pastoral support to people of all faiths and individual beliefs.

Now on to my next confession. Mark Roberts, or Marko as we referred to him, was a player who continually tried to wind me up. He would say things like, "Rev, if we get a penalty and I ask Satan to help me score – are you okay with that?" That was actually mild compared to some things he would say to try and get a reaction from me. One morning, shortly before Christmas, he finally got under my skin. Now, before I tell you this story, I need to tell you something very important so you will not judge me too much – I love dogs! We have had a pet dog for most of our married life and I consider them to be the most cute, friendly and faithful creatures on God's planet. I would never want harm to come to anyone's pet dog. I love dogs – I really do!

One morning, as we were approaching the Christmas period, Mark came in to the dressing room and said, "What's all this ******* babe in a ****** manger about. What a load of ******* *****." He did not mean it – he just wanted to get under my skin. Well, he did. Right under! You could tell the lads were sitting there thinking, "The Rev is surely going to bite on this one…" And bite I did – hard! I said something that I knew would get under *his* skin.

You see, although Mark had a girlfriend who he loved very much, the screensaver on his phone was a photo of his other great love, his Doberman, Jack. As much as I love dogs, I heard myself saying, with a serious face, though completely in jest, "Marko – I hope your dog dies!" Well, Mark was utterly shocked, it was the last thing he would ever have expected the Rev to come out with! Meanwhile, the rest of the dressing room fell about laughing. Some of the players started to tease him by singing, "The Rev's cursed your dog; the Rev's cursed your dog…" Someone put their arm round him and said very sombrely, "Marko, when you go home today, your dog will by lying on its back with its four legs facing upward – rigid – stone dead." As we jogged round the pitch during the warm up, Mark ran alongside me and said, "Rev I'm really sorry for slagging you but will you pray that my dog is okay? I'm really worried something bad might happen to him!" I told him not to worry about the dog, but inside I was praying, "Lord, please preserve that dog's life, I'll never live this down if he dies!" That afternoon at 2pm, I received a text from Mark, in block capital letters, "REV MY DOG'S ALIVE, THANKS FOR PRAYING!"

I replied back, half-jokingly, telling him to acknowledge God's goodness by pointing to the heavens if he scored the following day. Well, Thistle defeated Ross County 5-2 up in Dingwall. Mark scored, and after he did so, he dutifully pointed to the heavens – before being flattened by his fellow players as they celebrated.

My final confession is one that I am the most ashamed of. When you are in a dressing room environment, it is so easy to adapt to the culture and say things that you would not say in any other setting. The humour of a dressing room is probably the most crude and inappropriate I have ever heard, though you cannot help but laugh at some of the things that are said.

Here is the context. The players were talking about their forthcoming Christmas night out. I remembered hearing of some of the shenanigans from the previous year's celebrations. Let's just say that some of the guys had ended up in a spot of bother. So, out of the goodness of my heart, I announced to the dressing room that I would keep my phone on that night. If anyone found themselves in a difficult situation they could call me and I would drive into Glasgow from Kilsyth, pick them up, and take them home. Quite a magnanimous offer in my view. However, this was not enough for one of the boys. "Rev, can we not just come and stay at your house?" My reply was surely understandable, "No chance! I've got two teenage daughters so if you think I would let a bunch of drunk footballers stay in my house overnight you've another think coming!"

Seeing an opportunity for a wind-up, he said, "Ach you're not much of a Christian. If it was my Catholic priest, he'd let us stay no problem because he's a real man of God – unlike you! Aye and what's more, he's celibate, he doesn't need to have sex like you, that's cos you're a fake Rev." Now, most of my best friends are Roman Catholics, as are most of my wife's extended family. Trust me, there is not a bigoted bone in my body – I absolutely detest sectarianism. And I have the utmost respect for anyone who sacrifices the opportunity of being married to live a celibate life.

However, I was caught up in the banter, and I wanted to give as good as I got. So I retorted by saying something to the effect that I very much doubted if priests actually kept their vows of celibacy. Immediately, I regretted saying it, and I apologised straight away. But the toothpaste was out of the tube and there was no way I was getting it back in.

Of course, I had not meant what I said. Of course it was just for laughs. Of course anyone else in the dressing room might have come out with the same wisecrack and no one would have thought anything of it. But this was the Rev and for him this was completely out of order. Half the dressing room exploded into laughter – that would be the Protestant half – but the other half looked at me sternly, ruefully shaking their heads. I had crossed a boundary and there would be consequences. Of course, they were winding me up because they knew what I was really like, but I felt absolutely awful. At that point, the manager walked into the dressing room and the "offended" player jokingly said, "Gaffer, I'll not be signing next season, I didn't realise this was a sectarian club. The Rev's a bigot!"

The manager thought it was hilarious but that afternoon as I drove home, I was in tears. I really thought I had blown it. I had taken it too far. Was there any way back? Now, depending on your perspective, you may have different responses to this. If you are a current or former player, you are probably thinking, "Rev, you're taking yourself far too seriously, that's just standard dressing room banter." However, if you are not involved in football, you are maybe thinking that what I said was worthy of resigning as chaplain! Even now, I cringe just thinking about it. Some Rev me eh?

When I got home, I decided to write a letter of apology to the "offended" player. I put "offended" in adverted commas because he was not in the slightest offended. He thought it was hilarious that I was feeling so bad about it. In my letter, I wrote about how sorry I was and that I did not want to be the reason he did not sign for Thistle the following season. If I was a stumbling block to him being at the club, I would step down as chaplain. I reiterated how much respect I had for Roman Catholic priests who had chosen a life of celibacy out of sacrificial love for the Lord.

There was a Christmas party for players and families coming up so I would see him then. Then the thought struck me – I would also see his wife! She was such a lovely, devout Roman Catholic who I used to look after along with their two boys in the Family Room at every home game. If she knew what I had said, she would surely lose all respect for me? The night came, and, sure enough, when she saw me, she signalled for me to come over to her.

She had a stern face. I was expecting an absolute rollicking but I was shocked at what she actually said… "Mark, has he apologised to you yet?" Me? Has he apologised to me? I could not understand what she meant. She continued, "I saw that letter you wrote to him and I could see how upset you were and how much he must have wound you up to write that. Mark, he's a wee hypocrite, he's not been in the chapel since our two boys were baptised and I gave him what for when he told me what he'd said to you! I know what a sensitive wee soul you are!" With that, she called him over from the bar and gave off to him for not reassuring me. Hilarious as that was, it does not take away from the fact that I was out of order. So please have mercy on me, I am only human!

These are just a few of the many mistakes I have made as a chaplain, but I have made many more as a husband, dad and church pastor. I am anything but perfect so the reason I find it very easy to forgive others is that I have been forgiven so much myself!

CHAPTER 9

FOR IF YOU KNOW THE HISTORY...

"Aha, so now we know what your *big* team is", I hear you say. This will be totally lost on anyone who does not realise that the title of this chapter is the beginning of a Celtic song. Much to the chagrin of Thistle supporters, they are often asked whether their *big* team is Rangers or Celtic, known as the Old Firm. Most Jags fans I know are very balanced, they have a chip on both shoulders and feel equal disdain for both the Gers and the Celts! Personally, I have good friends who work with both clubs so I have no axe to grind against either side of the great Glasgow divide. I particularly like to see them both progress in European competitions as I do with all Scottish clubs. Having said that, on the rare occasion that Thistle enjoy a win against either of the big two, I must confess there is no victory that tastes so sweet!

The title of this chapter actually has nothing to do with mixed allegiances – it tells the remarkable story of how chaplaincy has grown exponentially in Scottish football over recent years.

I certainly cannot take the credit for being the first Scottish football chaplain. That honour probably goes to the late James Martin, affectionately known as Jimmy the Mini, who was long-time chaplain to Motherwell FC. Jimmy, a local minister, was friendly with the manager of the Steelmen in the 1950s and was invited by him to keep fit by joining the players on runs round the park. If there were any pastoral crises at the club, Jimmy was always on hand to offer his support.

Motherwell have experienced more tragedies than most clubs, with the passing away of club legends Davie Cooper, Phil O'Donnell, Jamie Dolan and Paul McGrillen. Jimmy was a great support to all concerned at the club in the aftermath of those bereavements.

When I became chaplain at Thistle, I was only aware of Jimmy at Motherwell and five other chaplains who were at Clyde, Dunfermline Athletic, Raith Rovers, Rangers and Stirling Albion respectively. None of us had received any formal training in sports chaplaincy. Jimmy Dowds was chaplain to Dunfermline Athletic and he became a great friend to me, a constant source of inspiration and encouragement. He heard that Manchester United had a chaplain called John Boyers. In 1999, Jimmy invited John to come up to Scotland and share with a small group of us about his own journey in football chaplaincy. That meeting at East End Park, home of Dunfermline Athletic, was to prove significant, as we formed a good connection with John, and subsequently, other English chaplains.

John became chaplain to Watford in 1977. Over the following years he pioneered chaplaincy elsewhere in English football, resulting in him founding a charity in 1991 called SCORE. This was an acronym for Sports Chaplaincy Offering Resources and Encouragement – the name was changed to Sports Chaplaincy UK in 2011. John became chaplain at Manchester United in 1992 and he continued to develop chaplaincy in football and also in other sports in England.

CONFESSIONS OF A FOOTBALL CHAPLAIN

As John shared how he delivered chaplaincy down south, we realised that we were basically doing the same job, we simply adapted the role to Scottish footballing culture. John himself acknowledged that football chaplaincy in Scotland needed "to have a kilt on it!" For a start, in Scotland we play down the "religious" element to the role. In England, at that time some chaplains turned up at games and even training sessions with their dog-collars and other clerical vestments – no way would that work in Scotland, it would just put a big barrier up. Instead, when I appoint new chaplains I encourage the club to give them team kit, by all means printing "Rev" or "Chaplain" on the training gear, so that people know what their role is. This is also what commonly happens in England now too.

John was a great support to us, making regular journeys to Scotland to encourage us. He also gave us a quote from the manager of Manchester United at the time – the legendary Scotsman, Sir Alex Ferguson. I have extensively used his commendation of sports chaplaincy all over Scotland as I have introduced the concept to clubs:

> *"Chaplains can be of help to all sorts of people involved with sport; when crisis, need or difficulty comes. I commend the idea of sports chaplaincy and the works of Sports Chaplaincy UK to you."*

The small group of Scottish chaplains quietly got on with their work at their respective clubs. I became friendly with Ray Montgomery when he played for a brief spell with Partick Thistle at the end of his career. Monty was a Kilmarnock legend having captained them to their famous

Scottish Cup win over Falkirk in 1997 – the first time they had won the trophy since 1929. It was no surprise that when Ray retired from being a player he returned to his beloved Killie to work behind the scenes. We continued our friendship and Ray mentioned that he thought it would be great if Kilmarnock had someone who did what he had observed me do at Partick Thistle.

So, in 2004, I met with Dave MacKinnon the CEO, and the management team of Jim Jeffries and Billy Brown, and I explained how I operated at Firhill. They agreed for me to source and train a chaplain for them. I approached someone who I knew very well. I had been to school with him, though he had been two years ahead of me. Neil Urquhart, a minister in Irvine, was very enthusiastic about the potential opportunity. Quite honestly, I cannot think of anyone who would have been a better first appointment. Neil was absolutely superb! He had the right personality, skillsets and experience – and he got on so well with every player and manager over a 10 year spell. I think he was the first chaplain to be christened "Charlie". I don't want to insult your intelligence by explaining how the nickname came about but if you are struggling to work it out, think of a famous silent film comic actor with a bowler hat and moustache. I refuse to give you any other clues! So I guess you could say that at this juncture, Sports Chaplaincy Scotland had begun. After his time at Killie, Neil went on to form an advisory board to see how the work of Sports Chaplaincy Scotland could be grown beyond football and he continues to be a great support to this day.

CONFESSIONS OF A FOOTBALL CHAPLAIN

Ray Montgomery had a good friend, Gus MacPherson, who at that time was the manager of St Mirren. We were introduced to each other and Gus opened the door for me to appoint a chaplain at the Paisley club. Again, I had the advantage of knowing what was available locally, as I had led a church in Paisley, called Hopehall, for 10 years. Hugh Chalk, the pastor of Mossvale Community Church, is still chaplain at St Mirren to this day, though with a lot more grey hair than when he started. At least he's got hair so let's move on!

Not long after this, I got to know Jim Fleeting who was the Scottish FA's technical director. I made an immediate connection with Jim, for me, one of the best guys in Scottish football. I found him to be an upright, compassionate person and a genuine family man. Jim loved the concept of chaplaincy and so he invited me along to speak at the UEFA A Licence coaching course to explain the basics and benefits of chaplaincy in football. At that time it was held at the Inverclyde Sports Centre in Largs. I met many different people from Scotland, but also from all over the world. For example, a number of great Portuguese coaches have obtained their coaching badges in Largs, such as Jose Mourinho, Andre Villas Boas and Nuno Espirito Santo.

Jim would introduce me by saying, "How would you like to have someone at your club who sorts out all your dysfunctional players – and it won't cost you a thing? This man will tell you about it and plus he'll provide that person for you!" And so I would deliver a seminar, which I entitled, "More Than Two Legs On A Saturday."

I would begin the seminar by saying, "If you only see your players as physical commodities, that's all you'll get. But if you give them mental, emotional and spiritual support, making them feel valued as a person, you might actually get a better player. And the chaplain can do that at your club - free of charge!"

It was unsurprising that quite a number of well-known retired Scottish footballers came up to me afterwards and said, "I wish our club had appointed a chaplain when I was a player!" Jim Fleeting was such a tremendous support to me personally. I regularly visited him in his office at Hampden Park and updated him on developments. If there was any club I wanted to speak to, Jim would have a contact there. He would phone them in my presence and say, "Here, I've got a wee pal and he wants to talk to you. He's a good lad, you'll like what he's got to offer – and it's free!"

Within four years of speaking at this annual course, I had sourced, trained and appointed around 16 chaplains at different clubs. Slow progress, but by 2011 we had 22 club chaplains in the SPFL, which proved to be a tipping point, as that was more than half the clubs on board.

I was really amazed at the growth, it was not something that I had ever imagined or planned when I became chaplain to Partick Thistle. However, it was becoming increasingly difficult to balance my work as senior pastor of Kilsyth Community Church and develop chaplaincy in Scottish football at the same time.

CONFESSIONS OF A FOOTBALL CHAPLAIN

By 2011, John Boyers had retired as head of Sports Chaplaincy UK, and Rich Gamble became the first CEO. Rich told me of a Welsh friend of his who was willing to finance me to be able to work two days a week to develop Sports Chaplaincy Scotland. The suggestion was that Sports Chaplaincy UK would pay my church for two days of my time and I would remain on the same salary from the church. My church had always been so understanding about the value of my work in football chaplaincy and they could not have been more supportive and encouraging. The leaders of the church were unanimous in agreeing to the deal. Since we had a lot of people who were able to share the load of my work, not least my wife Aileen, they agreed to release me for those two days a week. I was, and still am, very grateful to them for that. Over the next two years, the number of chaplains grew from 22 to 36 of the 42 clubs in the SPFL. Now we have chaplains at 40 of the 42. Scottish football was taking this seriously!

I met three people on the 2013 UEFA A Licence course who were to prove very significant in the next stage of growth for Sports Chaplaincy Scotland. Firstly, I met Ally Macleod who was, at that time, the assistant manager of Nairn County, who compete in the Highland League. Secondly I met Carlos De Angelos, who was a coach with Edinburgh University FC, soon to be founder members of the newly formed Lowland League. And last, but most certainly not least, I met Willie Kirk, manager of Hibernian Women of the Scottish Women's Premier League. Each of them asked if I could provide a chaplain for their respective clubs. I tell the stories of their appointments in other chapters and each account is worth the read!

Doors of opportunity to develop chaplaincy were now beginning to open far beyond the SPFL. However, there was no way I was going to be able to meet the increasing demand from Scottish clubs, even by working two days a week on it, so something had to give. Naturally, I prayed about it and asked God to show me a way forward.

That August, I was up in Dingwall with Partick Thistle, as we were playing Ross County. Their chairman is Roy MacGregor, a man highly respected throughout the game in Scotland and for good reason. What an incredible job he has done, leading the club from the Highland League to the Premiership, including a League Cup win!

Roy introduced me to someone who was his guest for the day at Victoria Park, the First Minister at that time, Alex Salmond. I was very surprised at the interest he expressed in the work of football chaplaincy. He asked if I would have a cup of tea with him and his wife at half-time and tell him more about the work. That I did and after I had shared how the work had grown he asked me what my vision was for the future. I told him that I wanted to see chaplaincy become available anywhere in Scottish football where people played the game seriously – be that the SPFL, Highland League, Lowland League, Women's Premier League or wherever else. "And what would it take for that to happen?" Alex asked. I boldly replied, "Funding for me to go full-time! Have you got any?" Thankfully, he laughed and said, "Well, I might have. Come and see me at Holyrood and we'll chat further about it. Give your number to my PA and she'll arrange something." I was gobsmacked, I did not expect this to happen.

I went to see Alex that October. By this time I had started piloting chaplaincy at Hibernian Women so I decided to go and see the First Minister in a smart light grey suit, wearing my Hibernian club tie. "So what?" I hear you say. Well, I knew this would test his humour and his willingness to help me because he is well-known for being an avid Jambo (Heart of Midlothian fan) – Hearts, of course, being the big Edinburgh rivals of Hibernian. My attire got the right response! When I walked in, he laughed, and said, "You expect me to help you wearing that thing?" He was joking of course, he did help me. He arranged for me to meet up with a government civil servant who secured me a year's funding, alongside funding from the Robertson Trust.

In January 2014, I stepped down from pastoring Kilsyth Community Church with their blessing. I had thought I was going to be with them for the rest of my life and I did struggle giving up my role there. However, there was a general recognition that I had to move on in order to meet the demand from football clubs throughout the nation. I had spent nearly 16 years focussing on equipping, empowering and releasing people to live their God-given dreams and fulfil their God-given potential, now it was my turn!

That next year saw 75% growth in the number of football club chaplains. A significant part of the progress was seen in the Highland League, where nearly every club invited me to source, train and appoint a chaplain for them. Ally Macleod, who had asked me for a chaplain at Nairn County, went on to be a great help in opening up doors to speak to other clubs in the Highland League. It covers a significant area in Scotland, the size of Belgium. To be able get round all these clubs to speak to their chairmen was quite a challenge but one I enjoyed enormously.

Highland League football is a great watch. It's like a throwback to the 1970s, there is no quarter given and no quarter taken. None of this passing the ball along the back four for five minutes, waiting for space to open up. I have never yet witnessed a 0-0 draw and every game I have watched has been highly entertaining. Also noteworthy is the wonderful welcome and hospitality at these clubs. The 90 minutes can be confrontational, at times even attritional, and that's just between the committee members of opposing teams! But the camaraderie before and after games is brilliant. There was a great openness among nearly all of the clubs to chaplaincy. I think the fact that they were being offered the same resources as SPFL clubs was a big factor in them being so receptive. I got the sense from many of them that they felt there was a central belt bias when it came to help for Scottish clubs, so I was glad to be able to try and change that perception.

During that year, the Scottish Government held negotiations with the Scottish FA and the SPFL. The footballing authorities, alongside the Robertson Trust, agreed to help fund my newly titled role as Scottish Director of Sports Chaplaincy UK.

CONFESSIONS OF A FOOTBALL CHAPLAIN

In January 2015, I was appointed as the Scottish FA chaplain. This entailed offering to source, train, appoint and oversee chaplains at all Scottish FA member clubs, serving as chaplain to the national squads as required, delivering workshops in the seven national performance schools and being pastorally available to any Scottish FA staff.

At that point, the professional game board of the Scottish FA insisted that I hand my role of chaplain at Partick Thistle to someone else. It was one of the hardest things I have ever had to do but it was the correct decision. It meant I was able to attend different games every weekend, giving me the opportunity to check that chairmen were happy with their chaplain's work. Football is such a fluctuating industry and it's important for me to meet every chairman and manager if possible. This means that if the club chaplain has to move on for any reason, I have a contact within the club to ensure a smooth transition in appointing a replacement. It also meant I could attend matches in leagues further down the Scottish football pyramid in order to introduce the concept of chaplaincy to other clubs.

As that season progressed, the new chaplaincy appointment was going well at Edinburgh University FC. I met Andrew Waddell, who was the chairman of the Lowland League at that time. He very helpfully allowed me to come to a meeting of club representatives and I was able to explain about chaplaincy to them. Perhaps the fact that nearly all of the Highland League clubs now had a chaplain was incentive enough for them to join the party. Within a couple of years, every club in the Lowland League had a chaplain.

One of the best things Stewart Regan did during his tenure as CEO of the Scottish FA was push for the pyramid system, similar to what has been so successful in England. The teams that win the Highland League and the Lowland League play off against each other and the winner of that two-legged affair has to play the team finishing bottom of League Two in the SPFL. The winner over two legs starts in League Two the following season. The pyramid has given clubs with ambition an opportunity to gain access to the SPFL and, in my opinion, the quality of football within the leagues outside the SPFL is excellent and continues to improve every season.

For me, what is happening in the tier below the Lowland League is the most positive development in Scottish football in my lifetime. Most Junior clubs have been moving over to the East of Scotland League and the recently formed West of Scotland League, with a view to seeking promotion to the Lowland League, and ultimately, the SPFL. If someone from outside Scotland is reading this, I need to explain that the term "Junior" does not refer to the age of the players. The closest equivalent terminology would be "non-League" football in England. The difference in Scotland is that historically, the Junior clubs did not want to be integrated into a pyramid system, they preferred to play other local teams and remain semi-professional.

Great credit should go to Kelty Hearts, who were the first club to make the move from the Juniors to the Seniors. Because of their tenacity, the future of the game in Scotland is really exciting in my view. And it also keeps me busy trying to find chaplains for the ever growing number of

CONFESSIONS OF A FOOTBALL CHAPLAIN

Scottish FA member clubs! At the time of writing, we now have 115 football club chaplains in Scotland. It is testament to the great work of our football chaplains that chaplaincy has also started to develop in other sporting contexts in Scotland such as rugby, cricket, shinty, basketball and in gyms.

As the number of football club chaplains grew, meeting with every club chairman over the course of one season proved to be too difficult but I was determined that quantity would not compromise quality. After considering various solutions, our East Stirlingshire chaplain at the time, Bill Sharp, made an excellent suggestion. He asked if we had experienced chaplains in each of the Senior divisions who ordinarily travelled to away games with their respective clubs. He suggested that they could check in with the chairman and chaplain of the home team. Following Bill's suggestion, I appointed divisional pastoral directors for the Premiership, Championship, League One, League Two, Highland League, Lowland League – and recently the East of Scotland League. The only challenge with this is promotion and relegation. If the club of one of the pastoral directors changes division it can be a bit of headache, but it's the best system we can think of just now with the limited resources we have. The directors report to me every quarter, letting me know what clubs they have visited and any issues arising. They also regularly check in with the other chaplains in their division. I continue to go to a different game every week and I am able to see each club every three years at least. I must be honest, watching a game as a neutral is far easier than when I was chaplain to Partick Thistle!

Sports Chaplaincy Scotland has officially been part of the Sports Chaplaincy UK family since 2011. Warren Evans became the CEO of SCUK in 2015 and he has been a delight to work with. He recognizes and respects the cultural and contextual differences in England, Scotland, Wales and Ireland and he is very careful not to impose an "English" way of operating. Each of the home countries has a national Sports Chaplaincy director and when we come together for directors meetings there is a genuine sense of unity. We all have an equal say in the direction of Sports Chaplaincy UK and our individual skill sets are made available to the other national leaders. In the words of the song that I quoted at the beginning of the chapter, "Oh it's a grand old team to play for...." Honestly, I'm not a Celtic fan – or a Rangers fan!

It was Stewart Regan's positive experience with chaplain Max Wigley when he was CEO of Yorkshire County Cricket that meant he was very open to facilitating my work in Scotland. In similar fashion, when Neil Doncaster was CEO of Norwich City, he had a good relationship with their chaplains Bert Cadmore and Arthur Bowles. So, when he became CEO of the SPFL, no one needed to convince him of the potential benefit of chaplaincy in Scottish football. So, I need to say with all humility, we in Scotland have greatly benefited from the good practice of sports chaplains south of the border. Credit where credit is due! A fair exchange, given that football as we know it today – a game involving two teams of players passing the ball to each other with the ultimate objective of scoring a goal – was first played in Scotland. And it was the Scots who introduced the beautiful game to England.

Yes, Scotland is the true spiritual home of football! No wonder Scotland supporters do not subscribe to the claims made in the lyrics of the 1996 England football anthem, "Three Lions." "It's coming home, it's coming home…" Really? I'm not sure about that my English friends! Scotland gave England football and England helped us establish football chaplaincy in Scotland — so we are even okay?

CHAPTER 10

MON THE WOMEN!

Developing chaplaincy in women's football was not something that I had ever considered. That was until I met Willie Kirk at the UEFA A Licence coaching course at Largs in May 2013. At that time Willie was the manager of Hibernian Women. To be honest, I was largely ignorant of women's football, though prior to meeting Willie, I had watched an excellent six-part documentary on BBC Alba about Glasgow City. Started by Laura Montgomery and Carol Anne Stewart, City are the most successful team in recent Scottish women's football history. The documentary identified Eddie Wolecki Black, their manager for 10 years, as the main reason for City's domination of the Scottish women's game at that time. I was really impressed with Willie Kirk's passion for the women's game and it was hard to turn down his request for a chaplain. However, when he asked if chaplaincy could be offered to his team, I had to be honest and say that I did not have a clue how to train anyone up for such a role. I did not know what the distinctive pastoral needs of a women's team would be. "Fine" he said, "Come and pilot it yourself!"

I agreed to come for a few months with a view to training future female chaplains for Hibernian and other Scottish women's teams. But I stayed for over two years, and when I finally moved on, it was a massive wrench. I loved the team. I was blown away by the players' technical ability, tactical awareness and physical fitness. I was also greatly impressed by their passion for the game and for the club. When I had been introduced to the players I said to them that, as far as I was concerned, they were every bit as much Hibs players as the men's team. There was certainly a number of players who were Hibees through and through and played "for the shirt" in a way that I have seldom witnessed in male players.

Getting involved with Hibernian Women opened my eyes to how over-looked, under-valued and under-resourced Scottish women's football has been. I came to respect and greatly admire the dedication of the coaching staff, players and everyone else connected with the club. The players may not have had a professional status but they certainly had a professional attitude. To train four times a week and then do strength and conditioning on top of that, demonstrated how committed they were to the game. The training sessions were superb and the games were so enjoyable to watch. I did not see diving or gamesmanship. They trained and played with a smile on their faces.

It really was a pleasure and an honour to be the first chaplain to a women's football team in Scotland, though I recognised that going forward it would be more beneficial having females as chaplains. The reason I say that is that I have two grown up daughters and, whilst I have a wonderful relationship with both of them, over the years there have been a number issues that they have spoken to their mum about rather than me. And to be honest, I have been quite relieved about that! My goal was, therefore, to find out first-hand what challenges would lie ahead for any other chaplains I appointed. I then planned to train up an army of female chaplains, so that I could offer exactly the same value and resources to the women's game as we had been giving to the men's game.

There are certainly different pastoral needs in the women's game. While some male players have too much time and money to know what to do with, and as a result some start gambling, the women had the opposite problem. At that time, they had to balance their footballing lives with work or study and, for the most part, they were paid nothing for playing the game. It simply was not an option for a female to play professional football in Scotland back then. Now, thankfully, a number of female players in Scotland have professional contracts, which means they do not have the same time pressures as before.

Another issue is that becoming a father does not generally affect a male player's career. Indeed, some of them sleep at their parents' house on a Friday night before a Saturday game so they are not disturbed by their recently born offspring. What if a female player wants to have children? Not only is her career put on hold, for many, having a baby has ended their career. They have to make much more of a sacrifice in order to play football and that is just one reason why I have come to respect and admire them so much.

I also noticed the difference in how they were coached. Willie and his assistant Chris Roberts were two of the finest coaches with whom I have worked. Willie moved on to pursue a career down south in the women's game. Chris took over as manager, in what was probably the most seamless transition I have witnessed. It was, therefore, no surprise to me that they eventually went back to working together, currently at Everton Women FC.

Both coaches recognised that it was so important to give the players confidence rather than lambasting them. In fairness to the players, they must have been a delight to coach. They had so much football intelligence. In my limited experience in management, I often found I had to give my players the same instruction several times until it finally sunk in – but with the females it seemed like you could give them several different pieces of information at the same time and it all sank in.

Moreover, the boys will slaughter each other in the dressing room and the rest will join in the fun, but the females will fiercely defend each other. At the first Hibernian Women game I attended, I was only able to arrive in time to watch the second half. The first half had apparently been a non-event, and the players had not been performing to their potential. In the second half they turned on the style and eventually defeated Rangers Women 4-1. As they warmed down, I strolled over to them to congratulate them and one of them said, "Thanks for coming to watch us, when did you arrive?" I jokingly replied, "Oh, I just turned up at half-time, the same as you lot did!" Tumbleweed moment. I have not tried to crack a joke like that since. It's not that they do not have a sense of humour but I have come to realise that there is a time and a place!

During my time with Hibernian Women, our arch nemesis was Glasgow City. We could beat anyone else in Scotland but there seemed to be a mental block when we came up against City. This led to many heart-breaking losses in the league and cups. Despite Glasgow City being our biggest rivals, their manager Eddie Wolecki Black became one of my best friends. We coined a phrase, "Enemies for 90 minutes, friends for life." When it came to training chaplains for other clubs in the Scottish Women's Premier League (SWPL), Eddie was a great help. He came along to our very first training day and painted a clear picture of the unique challenges facing female footballers in Scotland.

That first group of rookie chaplains presented a big challenge to me, in that half of them were absolutely clueless about football! This did not put me off training them because what mattered to me was that they were passionate about women receiving the same value and resources as men. I knew they were going to get right behind their teams and be their biggest fans. Part of their ongoing training was that they had to watch Match of the Day, Match of the Day 2 and Sportscene. There have been quite a number of husbands of female chaplains who have come to me, thanking me from the bottom of their hearts. Not only are they *allowed* to watch football on the TV as much as they want, now they are actually *forced* to do so! The female chaplains are also encouraged to watch the Women's Football Show, which covers the English Women's Super League, in which most of our national team play.

One of my first appointments was Karine Quinn, a Brazilian married to a Scot. She was surely bound to be savvy about football? You would think. Certainly, she would always watch her beloved national team play when they were on TV, and decorate her home with Brazilian flags. Well, she might have been enthusiastic about Brazil, but I'm not sure if she had much of an idea of what was actually happening on the pitch.

I appointed Karine at Celtic Women. Her first game was against my team, Hibernian Women. I explained to Karine that her team were playing left to right and encouraged her to get right behind them. To be fair, she certainly did that. With her strong Brazilian accent, throughout the game, she shouted, "Come on Gherrils….." a phrase for which she became renowned – that and the big hat she used to wear. People assumed it was just part of her Brazilian flamboyant character, but she actually had to wear it to shield her head and face from the sun due to a skin condition. So, if you were wondering why on earth someone would move from Brazil to Scotland, now you know!

Back to Karine's first game… All was going well, but in the second half she appeared to change her allegiance to Hibs. Okay, the Hibees were having the better of the game and were winning but how could she be so fickle? I said, "Karine, you need to stick with *your* team!" "I am!" she protested, "You told me my team were playing left to right." She did find it strange that Celtic had appeared to have changed their strip for the second half but she had not cottoned on to the fact that they actually switched sides at half-time!

She became very popular with the players and she was usually invited to anyone's birthday celebration. On one occasion a famous person came into the function suite much to the surprise and delight of the players. Clearly, the birthday girl and her teammates were desperate to have a photograph with this celebrity, so Karine thought nothing of waltzing up to the person and asking him to get in the photograph with the players. He dutifully obliged, but Karine could not understand what everyone was so excited about, so she innocently asked who he was. The birthday girl replied, "Who is he? Are you serious? That was Neil Lennon! Wow, now we really know that you support us because you love us and not because you love football!" To be honest I don't think Karine would have known Neil Lennon from John Lennon.

One final story I love from Karine's time at Celtic was when one of their players went down badly injured – that's obviously not the part of the story I like. When a female player goes down and screams in pain – you know it's for real. I have never come across any play actors in the women's game. The physiotherapist went on to the park to attend to her. Karine felt she should go on too, to try and give some comfort to the player. She took her hand and offered to pray for her. "Oh yes please Chappy!" was the response. Karine started to pray for her but as she did so, a teammate who had ran over to the scene started to cry, "Oh no Chappy, is she dying, is she dying?" Karine reassured her that the situation was not that grave, to which the relieved player said, in all seriousness, "Oh that's okay then, I thought you were giving her the last rites!"

As I mentioned earlier, I knew the time would come when a female would have to replace me at Hibernian Women. After my final game with them, they presented me with a huge box of chocolates and everyone had signed a beautiful card. I don't think I ever got that kind of send-off from Partick Thistle. Although, to be fair they did take me to Magaluf…

One of the players' dads came up to me to tell me his daughter was devastated that I was moving on. I was shocked to hear this, because she had never actually engaged me in a one-to-one conversation about anything. I enjoyed a bit of banter with her in a group setting with the rest of the players, but that was it really. I explained my surprise to her dad but then he said something that really made me think, "Yes I know, but she loved that fact that if she did ever need you, you were there, and that in itself was a great comfort and brought security."

When I appointed Catriona Lamont as chaplain to Hibernian Women, I must admit she took the standard of chaplaincy there to a whole new level. For a start, she brought in delicious and healthy tray-bakes to training to give her the opportunity to engage with the players one-to-one. They went down a treat. She also started to have the entire squad round to her house for dinner – I could not have competed with that! When Hibs have played in the UEFA Champions League, Catriona is seen as such an invaluable member of staff by the club that they actually take her away with them. The club's fortunes also improved as she saw the players overcome Glasgow City's dominance, at least in the cups. At the last count, she has witnessed seven triumphs between the Scottish Cup and Scottish League Cup. Of course, Catriona cannot take any of the credit for that! Despite Hibs' success in the cup competitions, City have continued to dominate SWPL1. At the time of writing, that is now 13 titles on the bounce – an incredible record. Their current manager, Scott Booth, has continued where my good friend Eddie finished off.

With Rangers and Celtic becoming professional, it remains to be seen if they can break Glasgow City's dominance.

The response to chaplaincy within the female game in Scotland has been encouraging. I try to attend women's games every Sunday during the season so that I can keep in touch with all the managers and check in with the chaplains too. On one occasion, I did not get the chance to speak to George Patterson, at that time the manager of Glasgow Women, so I phoned him the following week to ask for an update on how their chaplain, Inonge Siluka, was doing. I actually had to move the phone away from my ear because he was shouting so loudly, "Mark we love Inonge, don't ever even think about taking her away from us!" Even though the sport she had played was hockey, Inonge, originally from Zambia, had a great understanding of female team dynamics and so took to the role very easily.

While some of the female chaplains have been clueless about football before they took on their roles, this could not be said of Lorna Farrell at Queen's Park Women. As mentioned in "Acknowledgements", Lorna has worked as a sports journalist. Her finest moment must surely be her interview with the great Thierry Henry. It should be acknowledged that she was only one of a group of reporters trying to get a word with the great French player, but the bold Lorna saw her chance and seized it. However, she was so excited at getting this opportunity she completely forgot what she was going to ask him, and heard herself say, "Thierry, what *is* that aftershave you're wearing, it's gorgeous?" A great breakthrough for the feminist movement...

CONFESSIONS OF A FOOTBALL CHAPLAIN

Lorna is well qualified to empathise with anyone's struggles due to the challenges she has faced in her own personal life. In 2008, Lorna had a mesh implant which caused extensive nerve damage. In 2013, a corrective procedure left her even more disabled. She is presently consigned to a wheelchair. As a friend, it was awful seeing her in perpetual pain but she has been using her horrendous experience in such a positive way. She is part of a group of women who have been campaigning to ban the medical procedure of "mesh treatment" which has crippled so many previously healthy women. At last mesh is currently suspended from use in Scotland. Despite the physical challenges she faces, Lorna is an inspirational and hilarious public speaker.

One of her greatest joys is being chaplain to the female Spiders. Despite Lorna having physical restrictions and being in a lot of pain, I had no reservations about appointing her as a chaplain. She has more energy than most. Given all her experience working in the secular media, I had no fears about introducing Lorna to the players either. I knew that she would be able to connect with the girls quickly and would not be "preachy" or "ram Jesus down the girls' throats". I was confident that she would take a "softly, softly" approach.

The moment came for her to say a few words after I had introduced her as a former sports broadcaster. She started well enough, explaining that she was there simply to be a friend and a "listening ear." But then she got excited, and you know by now what can happen when Lorna gets excited... She blurted out, "I have to tell you something else about me,

...lly love Jesus who is totally awesome and has changed my life and I am not supposed to ram him down your throat, but seriously, he is so amazing and real and he loves you all… and I was such a screw up but Jesus totally forgave me and he'll do the same for you and I can't wait to be chaplain here and get to know you all"… To her left, I was putting my head in my hands, thinking, "Well all the best Lorna, now that they probably think you are a raving Bible thumper!" I should not have worried. She immediately endeared herself to the players and they were clearly not put off by her enthusiasm for Jesus. On one occasion, while travelling through to Edinburgh on the team bus, the players were listening to their music - a fine eclectic mix of dance music, hip hop, garage, grunge and the occasional George Ezra. Right in the middle of the playlist, an old hymn came on, "Oh Happy Day." They all started singing it, saying, "This is for you Lorna, a God tune!"

If you ever go to a Queens Park Women game at Lesser Hampden, Lorna will not be difficult to identify, and I don't mean because of the wheelchair. She will be the noisiest person in the ground – an incredible encourager of the girls. On one occasion, after a run of bad results, they were playing in an away game. Lorna screamed, whooped and hollered throughout the match and it obviously worked. They scored against the run of play.   She was ecstatic, cheering very loudly, even managing to do a wheelie. However, the coach raced up to her and said, "Lorna, what are you doing? It's a friendly and we don't cheer opposition own goals!" The players appreciated her encouragement nonetheless.

CHAPTER 11

MON THE WOMEN – THE MASTERS

I do appreciate that the title of this chapter may make you think I have finally realised who is in charge of the human race! However, I am actually going to be sharing the findings from research I conducted while studying for a Masters degree.

In many contexts, women still do not have the same opportunities, rewards and value as men. And this has certainly been true in football. "The future of football is feminine." So said Sepp Blatter, the former president of FIFA (Federation of International Football Associations), in 1999, in the aftermath of the Women's World Cup final. It's unclear as to what precisely Blatter meant by this comment, but he was probably predicting that the influence and involvement of women within global football would increase significantly.

Interest in women's football is definitely growing worldwide and, thankfully, also in Scotland. Our Women's National Team has qualified for the last two major international tournaments – the 2017 European Championships in the Netherlands and the 2019 World Cup in France – and this has really helped the burgeoning interest in female football in Scotland. But it has not always been like this.

In November 2016, I graduated with a Masters degree in Sports Chaplaincy at the University of Gloucestershire. In the words of the old TV advert, Carlsberg don't provide opportunities to study for degrees, but if they did… My time of studying coincided with me receiving first-hand experience of the challenges faced by female footballers in Scotland, as I was pioneering chaplaincy in women's football at Hibernian. So, for my final dissertation I decided to research "Issues surrounding Scottish women's football and the impact of chaplaincy." What an eye-opener it was to me – in two main ways. Firstly, in terms of discovering the historic treatment of Scottish women footballers. Secondly, from what I was told when I interviewed eight female national team players.

We will start with the history of women's football in Scotland. Football has long been a male bastion of Scottish society. The general opinions of male football supporters and the scarce publicity given to women's sport by the media have combined to cause Scottish women's football, on the whole, to be disregarded. The one Scottish male sports journalist who has been an exception to this is my good friend Alan Campbell. He has consistently championed Scottish women's football over the years and there is no doubt in my mind that he has played a significant role in our female game having an improved profile. Not everyone has been as supportive.

An example of this actually served to garner more support for the women's game. In September 2013, Tam Cowan, on his own admission, scored a spectacular own goal. He wrote a typical tongue in cheek piece in his Daily Record column which absolutely slaughtered women's football. I would not consider Tam to be a misogynist, his article was not meant to be taken seriously – but it certainly got the nation's attention. He was publicly vilified and even threatened – and that was just from his wife Liz! At least it brought women's football into sharper focus in the media. To be fair to Tam, he has made up for his blunder. He has had many female national team players on the "Off the Ball" radio show and now seeks to champion the women's game. I am sure he learned his lesson, as I did with the Hibernian Women players. Cracking a joke at females' expense is only funny if they find it funny!

The first records of football being played by English women date from the 19th century. However, the oldest reference to women in the UK playing football is contained in church records from Carstairs, Lanarkshire, Scotland, in 1628. The local church minister expressed his disdain at people from within his community, both male and female, playing football and thus violating the observance of Sunday as a day of rest.

Another historical account suggests that the first known football match in the UK between teams consisting entirely of females was in 1795, when two groups of Scottish fishwives – women who traditionally sold fish – played against each other.

In the 18th century, football was linked to a pre-marital tradition in the Scottish Highlands. Single women competed in football matches against married women. Single men would observe these games and choose potential brides based on their perceived footballing ability. Clearly, playing football was not considered to be an "unfeminine" pastime!

It seems likely that the forms of these aforementioned football matches would be similar to those historically played on Shrove Tuesday. On this day, a crude form of football was played by local people, which could best be described using the famous phrase of the much-loved Scottish football commentator, Arthur Montford – "What a stramash!" It usually resulted in many serious injuries and even some fatalities as a result of fighting and general lawlessness.

The first recorded football match that would have been similar to modern football, involving two teams of Scottish women, took place in 1888 in Inverness.

The first contest between two female teams that was played within Scottish FA rules was held at Shawfields Ground, Glasgow in 1892. The Scottish Sport newspaper reported on the event in a disparaging fashion, but it did not include any details of either the teams or the score. A football association for Scottish women was started in 1894. An attempt was made by organisers and participants to demonstrate that playing football and being ladylike were not incongruous!

The First World War provided the potential of being a game changer for women's football. While men were involved in military combat abroad, women were drafted into Scottish factories, often within the munitions industry, that would normally have employed males. Within these workplaces women were encouraged to play organised football matches as a means of raising finance for war charities, enhancing comradeship and encouraging their physical, mental and emotional wellbeing.

CONFESSIONS OF A FOOTBALL CHAPLAIN

The Dick, Kerr Ladies football team was formed at a munitions factory in Preston, England, during the First World War. They visited Scotland in 1921 and played Scottish women's teams in Edinburgh, Kilmarnock, Aberdeen, Dundee and Dumfries, attracting a total of 70,000 people. One of those games was played at Tynecastle Stadium, the home of Heart of Midlothian, before a crowd of 15,000 in March 1921. However, that same year the Scottish FA unofficially banned women's football teams from playing at its affiliated grounds because the organisation deemed playing football to be an unsuitable preoccupation for women!

This prohibition was upheld until 1973, yes 1973, when the Scottish FA rescinded the ban. In 1971, UEFA (Union of European Football Associations) invited its member national football authorities to vote on whether they should welcome women's football associations within their respective countries to come under their domain. 31 out of the 32 nations represented voted in favour of the proposal. The Scottish FA was the only European national footballing governing body who voted against it. After ongoing correspondence from UEFA, the Scottish FA formally recognised the Scottish Women's Football Association (SWFA) in August 1974.

Thankfully, we have come a very long way since then. In 1998, the SWFA became a National Affiliated Association of the Scottish FA and was subsequently known as Scottish Women's Football Ltd. The organisation was provided with offices at Hampden Park, the main headquarters of the Scottish FA.

CONFESSIONS OF A FOOTBALL CHAPLAIN

The Scottish Women's Football League was established in 1999. In 2002, clubs from within that association created the Scottish Women's Premier League. There are now 26 SPFL clubs and four Lowland League clubs with female teams competing in SWPL1, SWPL2 and the Championship. The latter is comprised of two regional leagues below SWPL2. Sports Chaplaincy Scotland has over 20 female chaplains now serving in these leagues.

There was a time when Scottish female players had to move to a different country in order to pursue their ambition to be professional footballers. In recent seasons, at least they have not had to travel too far away from Scotland, since they can play professionally in England. However, as I mentioned in the last chapter, Rangers and Celtic have become professional, and other Scottish clubs are aiming to do the same. Exciting times are ahead for women's football in Scotland, and I am delighted with the contribution our female chaplains have made during its development.

There is no doubt that the Scottish FA has demonstrated a much more positive attitude towards women's football in recent years by giving greatly increased recognition and resources to the women's game. On an international level, there have been great improvements in the provision of technical support, training facilities and playing kit for the national team. The association has also sought to advance the grass roots development of female football, by appointing a Girl's and Women's Football Club Development Officer in each of the six Scottish FA regions.

CONFESSIONS OF A FOOTBALL CHAPLAIN

The main part of my dissertation for my Masters involved interviewing eight national team players who, at that time, were still playing in the top flight of women's football in Scotland. Four of them played for the senior national team and four were part of the under-21 squad. They were all trying to balance their football commitments with study or work. None of them had the opportunity to play professional football in Scotland at that time. I wanted to find out how this affected their self-esteem, self-assurance and self-worth, and what impact chaplaincy was having on them in relation to these issues.

All of the players felt that one of the problems they faced was the historical perception of what a Scottish female footballer would look like. Descriptive words that sprang to their minds were: short, stocky, butch, cropped hair and unfeminine – whatever femininity actually means, who decided what it should look like anyway? All of them also said they thought there would be a general assumption that a female footballer would be a lesbian. Whilst it was considered a good thing that homophobia was not an issue within the female game, it was also widely acknowledged that it had been hard to attract and retain heterosexual women as a result of these perceptions.

On the subject of looking "feminine", the players felt they were faced with a dilemma: if they sought to look physically attractive, they were concerned that they would be objectified by spectators – looked at because of their physical appeal rather than their sporting ability and, thus, they felt they would not be taken seriously as footballers. However, they thought that if they did not take care of their appearance, they may be accused of reinforcing the stereotype.

Another issue was that the female game is often compared unfavourably with men's football. Men are usually stronger and faster than women. However, they are not necessarily technically superior to female players. The players I interviewed did not feel they were taken seriously as footballers. It's a perception not helped by the relatively small crowds, comprised mostly of friends and family, attending their games.

Though the players I interviewed had an amateur status, all of them felt that the amount of time, effort and work-rate that they dedicated to training and playing the game made them worthy of the status of "professional footballer". It was hugely frustrating to them that, despite their commitment, at that time, there was no prospect of them becoming recognised and paid as professional players in Scotland. Recently, it was refreshing to hear Dave King, the former Rangers chairman, speak honestly of how he felt that the female department of the club had historically been treated like "an unwanted stepchild". That certainly resonates with how these players felt.

Taking into account these issues of image, value and pressure, it was evident from the players that they felt chaplains were able to have a positive effect on their self-esteem, self-assurance and self-worth. The players recognised that they were valued by the sports chaplains to the same extent as their male counterparts regardless of their race, social background or sexual orientation.

Because of the intensity of relationships often found within women's football, they felt it was easier to talk to someone who was part of the club, yet also neutral – someone who could listen impartially and non-judgementally about their situations and give objective advice if required. The players all said they felt free to express their feelings, share their problems and talk about the pressures they were facing with the chaplains, more so than with other people from within their clubs, friendship groups or families.

We undertake to continually upskill our female chaplains in areas of pastoral work that are relevant to Scottish female footballers – issues such as self-harm, eating disorders and relationship conflicts. They are trained to understand the nature of these problems and know what measures to take in terms of signposting the players to appropriate professional help, while supporting them at the same time.

It has been heartening to see many SPFL clubs give more recognition to their female teams. I would love to see them do more to encourage their fans to get along and support the women. In my opinion, the main component that is lacking at the top level of the female game in Scotland is "atmosphere", and this is mostly due to small numbers of people attending. I do think there is a market for women's football – and that is young families. Many supporters complain about the price of men's football and the loutish behaviour of some fans, however, you will not find this at women's football matches. It can be a very entertaining watch, especially at the top end of the women's game. Anyone who attended games at Euro 2017 or World Cup 2019 would tell you what wonderful family-friendly tournaments they are too.

From a personal point of view, I am so glad I was introduced to women's football. I really hope that I, along with our female chaplains, can continue to have a positive impact on its development and recognition. Mon the women!

CHAPTER 12

NATIONAL TEAM CHAPLAINCY

Club chaplaincy is now well established in Scottish football but what about chaplaincy with the national teams? Part of my remit from the Scottish FA was to provide chaplaincy support to the national teams "as required". In 2015, I met with Anna Signeul, the Women's Team manager at that time, and explained that I was happy to offer my services to her. She simply said, "Well, I'm an atheist!" This is a response I have had from many people in the game. As usual I laughed and said, "Well, we all have to believe something, whether we believe in God or not, but that's not really what chaplaincy is about." I explained that we were equally available to people of all faiths and individual beliefs. I could tell she was still a little unsure, but as we talked, we soon began to realise that we had something in common. We were both passionate about the development of women's football in Scotland. Both of us shared the same dream – that Scottish girls would be free to live their dream of becoming professional players – in Scotland! Also, because Anna had her finger on the pulse of Scottish women's football, she was continually hearing great reports about the work our female chaplains were doing in the SWPL and she very quickly began to warm to me.

Whenever she organised training camps, she would invite me to come along for the day. I knew the Scotland-based players, so it was great to see them. Meeting some of the more experienced players who played down south or abroad was a bit daunting. I wondered if they were thinking, "We've never needed a chaplain before so why now?" I suppose it was going to be perfect timing because we had never qualified for a major international tournament but we were going to do so this time. I know some of the players really appreciated me being there. This backed up the research for my Masters dissertation, in which every national team player I interviewed said they thought it would be great to have a chaplain at training camps and tournaments. To quote one of them:

> *"A chaplain going away would probably help as… it can get quite stressful being away from home maybe or if the results are not going your way just having someone there to talk to cos obviously you're spending twenty four seven with your team and your roommate and stuff like that so it can get quite intense, so just having someone outside the team, obviously still part of the team, but as a neutral, would be good."*

At club level, a chaplain is seeing everyone twice a week, but in an international setting it was more of a challenge to build up relationships with people I had never met before and only saw once in a while.

When I started as Scottish FA chaplain, I was given training gear. However, when the new kit came out it was proving problematic for me to procure some. This meant I was turning up to national team training camps in the old gear, which did make me feel quite awkward. Anna asked why I had not been issued with the new kit and I did not have an answer for her. So, she disappeared for five minutes, and when she came back, she handed me all her personal kit – tracksuit, top, shorts – the lot.

This was in the days before they produced "female" kit. "Well they'll have to give kit to me", she said, "I'm the manager!"

The first Scotland Women's game I attended was a World Cup qualifier against Belarus at Motherwell's Fir Park stadium on October 23 2015. Jane Ross scored just before half-time and, as was my normal practice in any game in which I'm supporting a team, I jumped up and down celebrating. However, it was one of those awkward, tumbleweed moments – I was the only one on my feet, let alone jumping up and down. Embarrassing or what? I looked around me in anger. Why wasn't anybody else celebrating this goal, instead of just politely clapping? Scotland had scored for goodness sake! Because it was Scotland Women, did that make it any less meaningful and exciting than if Scotland Men had scored? Not for me! Scotland is Scotland, end of. Men or women – I do not make any distinction, except to explain which gender is actually playing. In terms of value and worth there is no difference to me. It was later explained to me that the reason no one celebrated exuberantly was that we would have been expected to beat Belarus – the game ended 7-0 to Scotland. And with only 1,000 supporters there, people would also have felt conspicuous by celebrating. I realised then, if I didn't know before, that there was a huge job to be done to get the Scottish football supporting public to buy into the female national team.

I particularly wanted to get the backing of the Tartan Army, the world-renowned group of Scotland supporters who are always likely to brighten up any international game or tournament.

When Scotland Women qualified for Euro 2017, their first major international tournament, I was so pleased for Anna and the players. One of my first moves was to try and galvanise support from the Tartan Army. I was just not sure how to go about engaging with them. How it came about was actually quite ironic.

I was with the men's national team at the Oriam, the national training centre based at Heriot-Watt University in Edinburgh. At one of the training sessions, a group of supporters had been invited to watch the squad train. I recognised one of them, Rory, who I had known for 18 years. I asked him if he was considering coming to the Women's Euros, and he said he was thinking about it. I then asked if he could tell me of any person of influence within the Tartan Army who I could contact. He explained that the Tartan Army is actually a big collection of autonomous, independent groups throughout the nation, but there was a group known as WESTA (the West of Scotland Tartan Army). Rory told me that one of the organisers within that group, Hamish Husband, might be worth connecting with. I contacted Hamish and another man Jim Brown, who had previously worked at Partick Thistle, so there was an instant connection. I explained that I wanted to encourage support for the national women's team at the forthcoming Euros.

They suggested that Anna come along to one of their group gatherings, which happened the last Sunday night of each month. I was going to be away on holiday with my daughter in Israel and Jordan, so I could not go with Anna but she went herself and spoke with great passion about her team. She received a very positive response.

The event even received back page headlines the next day in the Daily Record, the most popular Scottish newspaper, saying that the Tartan Army was going to back the women's team in the Netherlands. The ensuing support was more than the players hoped for I think, and that support has continued to gain momentum.

Anna said that she wanted to have me in her backroom team for Euro 2017, however, she did not have a budget to cover any expenses for me. I was very understanding of that. Chaplains do not want to be a financial burden on clubs and so they usually cover all their own expenses – this means we are not accused of being freeloaders and also enables us to retain our neutrality. Things are no different in international football, so I needed to find a place to stay in Utrecht, a beautiful city in the Netherlands, where the Scotland team were based.

I did not know anyone in the country, but I got in contact with an American friend who was the chaplain to female tennis players on the international circuit, working at the major tournaments with them. I cannot think why I thought she would have had any Dutch contacts but I asked the question anyway. As it happened, she knew one Dutch person, John. He knew another Dutch guy, Jan. He knew a Dutch girl called Nienke who lived in Utrecht, and she was going to be away for the summer. I was able to use her room and also borrow her bicycle to travel around the city. I stayed with my new friends Anne, Magda and Geke in Utrecht and visited the squad by cycling 45 minutes to the team hotel. I would then accompany officials to the training ground before returning back to the hotel with them.

It did feel a little bit like being an outsider – not really part of the staff – but it was also good to be available if needed. Sometimes as a chaplain you do feel a bit like a spare part. Although if your car breaks down, it's always good to have the spare part you require close by, so you can fix your car and get back on the road.

Our first game was against the "auld enemy" England. We got off to a bad start, conceding an early goal, and it was downhill from there, eventually losing 6-0. It was a hard loss to stomach, but the attitude of the girls after the game was great. They had to shrug off this defeat very quickly before our next game against Portugal and they did just that.

Two days after the England game, I visited the squad at the hotel and training ground. I felt that there was a couple of players who were in particular need of encouragement and I was able to draw alongside them and give them some reassurance. It is vital for a chaplain to always remain upbeat and positive regardless of results.

Also at the training ground that day were most of the coaches from the Scottish women's league clubs. They had been invited to come out for the first six days of the competition to learn as much as they could from visiting Ajax FC in Amsterdam, observing the national team training and analysing other games in the tournament. It was a fantastic learning opportunity and great credit to the Scottish FA for organising this.

It was also a good opportunity for me to spend time with the coaches and obtain appraisals of the chaplains' work with their respective clubs.

CONFESSIONS OF A FOOTBALL CHAPLAIN

I was invited to join them on their bus to travel to Scotland's second game against Portugal. All I had to do was cycle 30 minutes to their hotel. I checked the weather forecast and it indicated there would be rain from 3pm, so I decided to set off earlier, at 2pm, and arrive an hour before their 3:30 departure. Only it didn't quite work out that way. The weather forecast was somewhat inaccurate – a thunderstorm suddenly happened at 2:20, 10 minutes from my destination. At least it was only 10 minutes from the hotel – how wet can you get in 10 minutes? Apparently you can get very wet. Let me assure you that if I had jumped into one of the canals, I would not have been any wetter! It felt like someone had poured a bath full of water over me. But not just over me – over my phone too, on which I was depending for directions through Google Maps.

My phone stopped working. I had no idea what direction to go from there – and there was no one around from whom I could ask directions. Any sane human beings were sheltering somewhere away from this deluge! I went in the direction that I thought would be the right way – only it turned out to be in the opposite direction. Eventually, I saw a car that had stopped at a McDonald's drive-through and asked them for directions. I'm sure what they said was very accurate but retaining the directions was to prove impossible. I blame it on me being a man. Thankfully, I found a few other people along the way who were very helpful. I arrived at the hotel – soaked to the skin – just as the football coaches were leaving. Not one item that I was wearing was dry – including my boxer shorts.

Donald Gillies, at that time, the Scottish FA's Head of Girl's and Women's Football, could see I was in no state to get on the bus. He very graciously gave me a spare pair of shorts and a top to wear. A really kind gesture – only they were several sizes too big. Added to that, I had to "go commando" because my boxer shorts were soaking, and so, as you can imagine, I felt quite vulnerable!

I arrived at the stadium, feeling conspicuous in my vastly oversized shorts and top. I was chatting to some of the coaches when I felt someone massage the back of my neck. I turned round to be warmly greeted by my good friend David Hamilton, who is the Scottish Government's Football Lead. After embracing, he suggested I come with him to greet the minister for sport, Aileen Campbell. Despite my protestations, because of my rather outsized outfit, he insisted that I came over to say hello to her. What I did not realise was that all manner of other dignitaries were there too. Imagine turning up at the Queen's Tea Party in your pyjamas and it will give you an idea of how I felt.

The game ended in a gut-wrenchingly disappointing result, a 2-1 defeat to Portugal. However, I was able to celebrate Scotland Women's first goal in a major tournament, and celebrate I did. Well, I lost the plot actually, and such was the exuberance of my celebration – no my shorts thankfully did *not* fall down – the TV cameras focussed on this delirious bald, bespectacled, bearded guy!

I visited the team hotel and training ground two days after the game, which was also two days before the next game. That way I felt I was not interfering with the post-match analysis or the next pre-match preparations. The players were also free in the afternoon and some of them were able to meet up with family and friends. It gave me the opportunity to talk to a number of players who I felt were in particular need of encouragement after the first two games. Obviously, it is not a chaplain's place to focus on the performance of players, but we can talk to them about how they feel the result or performance has affected them mentally or emotionally. I had good talks with some players, who seemed to really appreciate the encouragement. What was also great was that there was a table tennis table set up in the hotel. I was able to play most of the afternoon with various players and also Anna the manager, who was a tremendous player and was unbeaten – that is, until I took her on. I am far too humble to tell you whether I won or not!

And so to the last game of the group stage of Euro 2017. Despite our heavy defeat by England and our narrow loss to Portugal, amazingly, we were still in with a chance of progression to the quarter finals. We had to defeat Spain in our last game by two goals and hope England defeated Portugal – which they went on to do, 2-1. No mean feat though – Spain were ranked higher than us and we were 18/1 to beat them.

That night will go down in my memory as one of the most heroic performances I can ever remember a Scottish team delivering – male or female. The players were tremendous. Spain had 74% possession to our 26%, 29 shots to our 6, 9 shots on target to our 2. The Scottish players were on the back foot for much of the game, under intense pressure, but they defended for their lives, literally throwing themselves at some shots.

When they could break up the park, they did. And on one occasion it led to a goal by Caroline Weir. What a celebration! I had never experienced anything quite like it. We had already scored our first goal in a major championship but this was the first time we had taken the lead – and against all the odds at that.

I confess I lost the plot even more than when we had scored against Portugal, as did everyone around me – it was incredible! For me, there were consequences. At one point as I was jumping, I felt like someone had taken a baseball bat and whacked my calf. I looked behind me but no one was there. No one had struck me at all, I had absolutely wrecked by calf muscle in my celebration and I had to crawl back to my seat in agony, where I remained for the rest of the match. Sadly, Scotland were not able to score a second goal to take them through to the next stage of the tournament but they still won the match 1-0 and showed the world what they were all about. I could not have felt more admiration for these players.

The first-aiders did their best to strap my calf but getting back to the train station with Geke, my Dutch friend, proved to be quite a challenge. Ultimately we did not arrive home until nearly one o'clock in the morning. I would like to say at this point how much I appreciated the wave of "sympathetic" posts on Facebook over the next day… At least lots of people had a good laugh at my expense, but I am used to that as a chaplain! Sadly, I did not get a chance to see the team after the game to personally thank them for their efforts, but I know they were really touched by the number of Tartan Army faithful, male and female, who turned out to support them.

When Anna stepped down as manager after Euro 2017, I knew that I did not have the capacity to continue as chaplain, due to my ever increasing commitments working within the field of mental health. It was with great sadness that I had to tell the new manager, Shelley Kerr, that I could not continue coming to the training camps. Having said that, I remain in contact with a number of the players and have been able to give pastoral support to them as the need has arisen.

I was definitely not going to miss the opportunity of supporting them when they qualified for the World Cup in France in 2019. It was good to catch up with a few of the players whilst there, and since I know most of the parents of the players, I was able to meet with them too, which was great. The Scots were very narrowly defeated by England and Japan and then an agonising draw with Argentina meant that the tournament was to end in disappointment, but the team has definitely shown that they belong on the world stage.

CHAPTER 13

THE ROSEY POSEY

I have mentioned elsewhere in the book about how much of a challenge it can be when you are chaplain to the club you have always supported. However, I countered that by explaining that even if you have no historic allegiance to a team, as you begin to work with them, you develop a deep love for them. That was certainly the case for me at Hibernian Women. I had no previous connection to the Easter Road men's team, nor did that develop when I worked with the women's team. Partick Thistle was my men's club and it would have felt like a form of footballing adultery to switch allegiance elsewhere. But does that mean I could never be a chaplain for another male football club? I was about to find out in 2018.

I was not allowed to be a chaplain to a Scottish FA member club due to potential "conflict of interest". That, of course, meant I could not work at any SPFL, Highland League or Lowland League club. However, the East of Scotland League, in the sixth tier of Scottish football, directly below the Lowland League, began to welcome many East Region Junior clubs into their set-up as part of the developing Scottish League pyramid structure. There was a growing interest among their member clubs in chaplaincy because many saw the appointment of a chaplain as part of their drive towards professionalism.

One of those clubs was Bonnyrigg Rose Athletic FC. The Rosey Posey are perhaps best known for being the football club that the famous actor Sean Connery played for. Connery turned out for the Midlothian side in

154

the early 1950s and is best remembered for scoring a cracking goal from 30 yards during a Scottish Junior Cup tie in 1951 against Broxburn Athletic. I cannot be sure, but I think the number on the back of his shirt was 7… The Rosey Posey did not go on to win the trophy that year, but they were winners in 1966. It's interesting, when you speak to Bonnyrigg supporters, they don't mention the 1966 win at every opportunity, unlike fans of a certain national team that also won a small trophy that year… Bonnyrigg won the Scottish Junior Cup for a second time in 1978. Now that *was* a memorable year for international football! Ah, Archie Gemmill's incredible goal for Scotland against Holland in the World Cup finals in Argentina. Surely, the most sublime moment of any World Cup, though perhaps the winners of the 1966 tournament might disagree.

I digress. I had placed a chaplain with Bonnyrigg Rose, but he was not able to continue with them, so, at my wife's suggestion, given that we were now living only 20 minutes from their ground, I offered to step in.

They welcomed me with open arms and I am so thankful for the opportunity to serve them for what was a fairly brief period of a year. It was great to be back at the coal face again. I had really missed having the training gear and boots on, even if it was only to kick the balls back into play when they had gone astray. It also gave me an insight into what it was like to be chaplain to a part-time men's team, as opposed to a full-time set up like Thistle. Given that the vast majority of future appointments are going to be with part-time clubs, I felt this would be great experience for me.

The manager, Robbie Horn, and his coaching staff Davie, Sean and Michael, were all so friendly. I already knew Sean as I had taken him on one of my regular trips to Rwanda, as part of a football coaching team. It definitely helps if you have a connection with someone from the club before you get involved, as that person can hopefully validate you and recommend you to the rest of the group.

One of the first challenges I had to navigate through was the limited time available to spend with the players in order to build those crucial relationships of trust. At Thistle, I would come in first thing on a Friday morning, train with the players, have lunch with them and usually leave about 2pm. On a Saturday I looked after their families or, if it was an away game, I travelled with them on the team bus. There were, therefore, plenty of opportunities to get to know the players.

At Bonnyrigg, this was not going to be so easy. Firstly, I was only able to attend one match a month as I had to go to different games each week around Scotland in order to check in with chairmen and chaplains, fulfilling my role for the Scottish FA. The second challenge was that, in common with the vast majority of male part-time clubs, the squad only trained two nights a week. They arrived at Lasswade High School, trained and then went home, so opportunities for a chat were scarce. Then I discovered that before training most of them congregated at the club for physiotherapy treatment and to play table tennis – ideal!

You will remember my story of taking on the mighty, previously undefeated, Anna Signeul at Euro 2017 in the Netherlands? Of course,

I didn't tell you the outcome of that match but I would hardly have mentioned it if I had lost...

Here was an opportunity to demonstrate my table tennis prowess to the Bonnyrigg players. The first two lads to arrive played against each other. The winner stayed on to play the next challenger. The winner of that and any subsequent games stayed on until we had to go off for training. So, I thought if I came early, and played first, I could enjoy a good half an hour playing table tennis, seeing off all comers, thus gaining respect from them. Except, I had not taken into account that just about all of them would be much better than me. I was defeated in most games, rarely getting more than two games a week! I had put that down to the fact that they were playing with decrepit, sub-standard table tennis bats so I replaced them with decent ones, if only for me to have more of a chance. While grateful for the kind gesture, some of them insisted on still using the old "half the rubber flapping off" bats – and I still got hammered most nights. Footballers are usually fiercely competitive at *everything* they do. It would not matter if it was tiddlywinks they were playing – they would still try to win at all costs.

The other way in which I was able to connect with everyone was by being added to the WhatsApp group of management and players. This meant that everyone had my number if they needed me and I had theirs in case I felt someone needed some pastoral support. It was also a good way of being kept in the loop if there was a change to training schedules or games. This is a normal communication mechanism at most clubs now, and I recommend that they include the chaplains in these groups in order to keep them updated. In some cases, clubs also have a separate "players only" group chat. It's maybe not such a good idea for the chaplain to be part of that WhatsApp group – unless you don't mind your phone pinging at 2am on a Sunday morning!

At the age of 55, there was no way I was going to join in the training sessions as I had done at Thistle, but I was able to retrieve stray balls during shooting practice. No mean feat, I can tell you! I lost count of how many vehicles in the school car park I had to crawl under to collect balls. I would do what I could to ensure that the full complement of training balls was collected in at the end of the night.

I thoroughly enjoyed observing the coaching sessions – the standard was superb. They trained as they played, nearly always with the ball – a great emphasis being placed on possession and movement. It was no wonder that they were such a joy to watch on match days. In some games in the SPFL, you can sense the tension and fear, particularly if a club is lurking near the relegation spots. Perhaps it is because there is not so much at stake financially in the leagues below the SPFL, but there certainly does not seem to be the same fear factor. I only had one full season with Bonnyrigg Rose but what a season it was. I will never forget it.

The East of Scotland League had attracted so many clubs from the East Region Juniors that they had to split into three conferences. Bonnyrigg had to win the inaugural Conference B and then, having won their section, play in a round-robin against the winners of Conference A

(Penicuik Athletic) and Conference C (Broxburn Athletic). Any critics of this set up would be silenced by what turned out to be one of the most dramatic play-off scenarios I have ever witnessed.

In the first game, Penicuik defeated Broxburn 3-2 and so they knew a victory against Bonnyrigg would see them crowned EOSL champions. However, Bonnyrigg prevailed, beating the Cuikie 2-1, thus setting up a massive game against Broxburn. This match still gave all three clubs a chance to win the play-off round-robin.

If Bonnyrigg drew with Broxburn or defeated them, it would be straightforward – the Rosey Posey would be champions. If Broxburn won 1-0 or 2-1, Penicuik would be champions. However, if Broxburn won by two clear goals they would be champions. Are you still with me? At various stages of the match, each of the three clubs stood to be crowned as champions. Only one prevailed in the end.

Broxburn went 1-0 ahead. At this stage Penicuik were in the driving seat, having scored the most goals. Then disaster struck – at least from a Bonnyrigg perspective – sorry but my Scottish FA neutrality was completely out of the window by this stage! Our goalkeeper was sent off for handling the ball outside the box. From the resultant free kick, Broxburn went 2-0 up – and now they were in the driving seat. If the situation stayed the same, they would be crowned champions of the EOSL.

Down to 10 men, many players carrying injuries, all of them exhausted from the marathon of the season and 2-0 down, any other team may have capitulated – not the mighty Rosey Posey! They managed to drag themselves back into the game by making it 2-1. Any Penicuik supporters who were at this game would have been celebrating once again, as, at this stage, the Cuikie were back at the top. Incredibly, Bonnyrigg then scored an equaliser – it was now 2-2 and for the first time they were in the driving seat. If they could just hold on! However, "hold on" is not a phrase I had come to associate with this team. No, they only believed in winning, and so they pressed for a winner – and it duly came, sparking incredible scenes on and off the park. The club posted online video footage of the celebrations that ensued after the third goal was scored. If you ever watch it, you will see the back of a wee baldy head bobbing along the bottom of screen – that will be me jumping up and down sideways! Bonnyrigg Rose Athletic FC were now the undisputed Kings of the East! And what an advert for the East of Scotland Football League.

The club had applied for an "entry level licence" and resultant Scottish FA membership. They were sure that they had everything in place to meet the criteria required, so everyone at the club began to celebrate in anticipation of competing in the Lowland League the following season. Only, it didn't quite work out that way. The criteria changed. Floodlights were now required, and, because they had only received 12 hours' notice of this requirement, Bonnyrigg had no chance of having them in place in time. Through some remarkable fund-raising efforts, money was raised to erect the necessary floodlights very soon after this, but the deadline had passed and it looked like all their labour was in vain.

Thankfully, the Scottish FA acted with sporting integrity and recognised that the timing of the change of criteria had given Bonnyrigg Rose no chance of complying with it. They eventually conceded that it was only fair for Bonnyrigg to be given their licence, membership and, most importantly, entry to the Lowland League.

During the period when they were looking for funds to erect the floodlights, I was desperate to be of practical help. I am not exactly a man of great financial means so I was not in a position to put money into the club, but I wanted to do something to help them raise funds. One morning, as I was having my daily devotional time of Bible reading and prayer, I was reminded that I had in my possession a signed Liverpool top from 1985.

Most people have a favourite English team and mine is Liverpool, not because I am a glory hunter, but because my mum was born across the road from Anfield. Even though Everton were the original tenants, from 1884 until 1892, it was Liverpool's ground long before my mum was born in 1931 – so the Reds were my team. This signed Liverpool top had been gifted to me by someone as a thank you for support I had given to her son who was a footballer. I had always been willing to let my prize footballing possession go, if money could be raised from its sale or auction for a good cause. I was reminded that morning that this would be a great time to sell it, given that Liverpool were flying high that season. I gave it to the club, they framed it, and managed to make some money by auctioning it.

CONFESSIONS OF A FOOTBALL CHAPLAIN

The drama surrounding the gaining of Scottish FA membership was an emotional roller coaster for all concerned. Now that this had been resolved, the club was overjoyed and so was I, despite knowing that this also meant that I would have to step down as chaplain. This was because I could not be aligned with a Scottish FA member club. Ian Maxwell had been managing director of Partick Thistle when the Scottish FA insisted I had to leave Firhill. Now he was CEO of the Scottish FA, so for consistency, it was clear what decision had to be made. To be fair to Ian, he give me a few months to find a replacement.

The club probably would not have realised what an absolute wrench it was for me to have to move on. They presented me with a lovely bottle of wine and a Bonnyrigg Rose top, signed by the players, which I will always treasure. I will look back on my time with them with tremendous fondness. They are a truly great bunch of people - the committee, coaching staff, physiotherapist and players. And I will always look out for their result – after I have found out the final score from the Thistle game!

CONFESSIONS OF A FOOTBALL CHAPLAIN

MIDDLEWORD BY EDDIE WOLECKI BLACK –
WORKING WITH THE CHAPLAIN

In 2013, as manager of Glasgow City, I was in the dugout in Edinburgh as we took on Hibernian Women in a vital league clash. There was great rivalry between Hibs and City because they were our closest challengers for the title. As it was, we managed to gain a narrow victory and consolidated our lead at the top of the table. I briefly spoke with the players after the game and made my way to the lounge for after-match hospitality.

It's always easy to enjoy post-match food after a win, however, as I was milling around the room chatting with familiar faces, I suddenly saw this small bespectacled man purposely coming towards me. My apprehension soon faded as he extended his hand and introduced himself to me as the chaplain for the Hibs Women's team. We gathered our food and sat down at a nearby table. As we were eating, I soon discovered this man had a great love of women's football and, just like me, had a long-standing faith in the Lord. We exchanged numbers and agreed to catch up in the not too distant future. Of course, it was a given that we would meet up when our teams renewed their on-pitch rivalry. I recall driving home that night mulling over our conversation and in all honesty he had left an indelible mark upon me. I knew I just had to remain in contact with this guy. The chaplain turned out to be Mark Fleming and it is fair to say that whilst we have been in opposite camps on the pitch, off it we have become the best of friends.

I regard Mark now as someone I would confide in if I was looking for an unbiased piece of advice. Our wives have also struck up a great rapport and we have hosted each other for meals several times over the years.

When I think back to our original meeting it does seem a little strange that we hit it off so well straight away. My view is that, above anything else, we both valued the three 3 F's – faith, football and family. We found a common ground there.

In my opinion Scottish football is better off for the involvement that Mark and his team of chaplains bring to the sport. Such has been his influence, wherever I go in Scotland to see a game of football, more often than not I bump into a chaplain representing one or both of the teams in action. I can also say, with knowledge, that Mark has made a big impression in the boardrooms of many of our clubs. To attain that level of trust that he has with people of high position speaks volumes for his integrity, humility and passion. I am under no illusions that it has been very difficult at times for Mark to break down certain barriers that hold this country back. Despite this, Mark has managed to achieve success through perseverance and patience. And as the Bible states, where there is perseverance, that develops character and that in turn produces hope. Therefore, the name in my phonebook that I have attributed to Mark is, "Man of hope". I cannot think of a more apt title to sum up Mark.

I terms of my own experience of chaplaincy, I will begin by sharing about my darkest moment in life, let alone football. Having enjoyed great success with Glasgow City in the women's game, I was keen to see if I could make it in the men's game.

After a successful spell at Edusport Academy, I was handed the reins at Airdrie in League One. I was given the simple remit of getting the team into the top four, which of course meant that the club would be involved in the play-offs, thus bringing in much needed revenue and the opportunity of moving up into the Championship. We had managed to achieve a run of victories, which saw us climb the table. Dunfermline were the team who were setting the standard, they were on a run that had seen them go unbeaten at home for more than a year. However, in a televised Friday night game, we went to East End Park and defeated them 1-0 in a well-deserved victory. As the season drew to a close, Airdrie were still very much in the mix for a play-off spot.

We made the journey to Cowdenbeath on 5 March 2016, and that date will remain with me forever. We made a decent start to the game and went ahead through a Jordan Thompson wonder strike. As half-time approached, I told my staff that I was going to the toilet. Once inside, I tried washing my hands but I could not turn the tap on. The physiotherapist, Kirsty, was nearby and I mentioned to her that something was wrong. She immediately contacted the doctor on duty and he very quickly diagnosed that I had had a suspected stroke. It turned out I had suffered a massive brain haemorrhage and my life was left hanging in the balance.

My wife Emma, who was six months pregnant at the time, came to the Edinburgh hospital with me. The curtains were pulled around my bed. Neither Emma nor the consultant realised that I could hear every word they were saying to each other. Emma naturally asked, "How is he going to be?" The consultant's reply hit me like a ton of bricks, "If he gets through the next 48 hours he will be lucky to walk or talk again". I had been developing a personal relationship with God prior to this situation, and it's fair to say that my faith really kicked in during those ongoing days. There was little hope being offered to me from a medical perspective, my prognosis was very poor – only God could help me now and I knew it. God did indeed help me and I continue to make a remarkable recovery, far beyond what was originally thought possible by the medical experts.

Ironically, Airdrie moved into fourth place in the table that dreadful day, having won the match against Cowdenbeath 3-1. Whilst I had been on course to deliver the required objectives of the club, it was clear that I was not going to be able to return to the club as manager that season.

Mark was a very significant person during that crisis in our lives, as was the Airdrie club chaplain at the time, Dave Brackenridge. He gave us incredible pastoral care during our hour of need and we remain close friends with him. Dave regularly visited me, bringing Emma in with him too. Dave was a continual source of encouragement and inspiration, playing a major role in helping me get back on my feet. It obviously helped that Dave had already built a great relationship with me at the club.

CONFESSIONS OF A FOOTBALL CHAPLAIN

Dave was a popular visitor to the dressing room, but it was not because of his footballing ability. He was the lead singer in a Christian rock band, the Royal Foundlings. He gave the squad a copy of one of the band's CD's and it was played regularly in the dressing room. The band were quite well-known in different parts of the world, playing in front of many thousands. With his long hair and beard, Dave did not have the usual look for a chaplain but, to be fair, he did look more like Jesus than any of the rest of them!

During my time as a manager in football I have been fortunate to have some wonderful chaplains as allies and I would like to go on record and pass on my heartfelt gratitude to each and every one of them. So, in no particular order: Sharon, Dave, Ruth, Karine and Jennifer – I thank you all so much for making my job easier than it should have been. Of course, I must also include Dave Ramage, who is the men's chaplain at Motherwell and who makes it a welcoming environment for all associated with the women's team when we visit the stadium. Finally to my good friend, colleague – and at times mentor – Mark Fleming, you're a star sir, and I thank you from the bottom of my heart.

I know that when Mark studied for his Masters degree, he wrote his dissertation on Scottish women's football and I believe his findings may very well impact upon the game for many years to come. If our national team progress to the finals of the European Championships, it will be the third major tournament in a row for our country, a record that can only remain a distant dream for our men's team.

I have no hesitation in saying that many people have played a significant role in that success, and I would say that the structure Mark has put in place throughout the length and breadth of Scotland is as significant as any others.

You see, in my opinion the role of a chaplain is to help keep harmony in the dressing room. I don't know anyone who likes working in an environment that lacks the space for growth, or where laughter is seen as a person lacking professionalism. I like my dressing room to be busy and loud, even if that means the chaplain takes control of the music. Also, if they are quick-witted without insult, then they are for me. I know there are some sceptics who view the presence of a chaplain in a dressing room as a no-good "Bible basher". That is certainly not my experience.

When I join a club, my chaplain becomes part of the backroom staff with access to classified information. My reason for this is simple, if the chaplain is aware that a certain individual is about to be left out of the starting eleven, they can use their expertise to ease the blow and get the player back onside and supporting her teammates. This has occurred in the past and the chaplain played a significant role in developing a positive environment for all concerned, whether they were a player or staff member. I don't think there is a more powerful statement a club can send out to their opponents than the substitutes' bench warmly applauding and encouraging their teammates during a game – and that is something that the chaplains model superbly!

CHAPTER 14

HOW DO YOU APPOINT YOUR CHAPLAINS?

I am often asked how and from where I manage to recruit chaplains. Obviously God is my main source of guidance but it also helps that I have very good connections with churches all over the nation, and that Scotland has a relatively small population.

Let me start by pointing out that just because someone is a church minister in the vicinity of a football club, it does not mean that they are necessarily the right person for the role of club chaplain. There are some clergy I have come across who do not have the right personality for such an environment. In one situation, I did not have much of a choice about who to appoint because the local minister had already "told" the club board he was going to be their chaplain. While they were a bit taken aback by his alacrity, they accepted him. However, from all accounts he was a law to himself. Because the club "was in his parish" he appeared to assume that he had the authority to go into the boardroom or the dressing room whenever he liked. He eventually moved far away from the area and I was able to appoint another chaplain there who has done a tremendous job, within the boundaries that the club has set! And this is how our chaplains should behave. We are conscious that we are at our respective clubs by invitation, we have no right to be there. We have no desire to impose ourselves on any department of the club. We go where the doors open to us and we do not go where the doors are shut. We are simply there to serve as required.

CONFESSIONS OF A FOOTBALL CHAPLAIN

Not all of the chaplains are church ministers/pastors. There are probably a number of reasons for this, but one of them is that ministers are often burdened with extra responsibilities beyond their church, like being on committees and looking after other churches. Added to that, most clubs in Scotland are part-time and only train midweek in the evening. You can imagine that this makes it very difficult for ministers for whom evenings are often the only time they can meet with people from their churches. However, while being a full-time clergyperson is certainly not part of the criteria for a being a football club chaplain in Scotland, every chaplain is required to have certain pastoral skillsets and experience.

A potential advantage to a chaplain not being a minister, but having what people would consider to be a "normal job", is that it challenges the perception that their role is a religious one. Add to that, a lot of the non-clergy chaplains are able to bring skillsets from their everyday work into the football club and this can enable them to be of even more practical benefit. Using people who are not clergy for this role perhaps means that ongoing training and support is all the more important, but I have found this development has been a very positive one.

If a chaplain has a job outside the church, this can sometimes make conversation easier. For the most part, players will not have had any experience of a church so if they can connect with you on something unrelated to chaplaincy, this can aid building relationships. Sometimes chaplains are already known to players. This can be helpful but also potentially embarrassing. When our chaplain at Elgin City, Gordon

Methven, was appointed and introduced to the players, one of them said, "Wait, I recognise you but I can't think from where." Half-way in to training, it dawned on the player that Gordon had actually arrested him when he had worked in the police some years previously. At least that chaplain will be guaranteed a bit of respect there!

So how do I source, interview, train and appoint chaplains? Sometimes I find them through the most unexpected of circumstances. For example, I was on the lookout for a chaplain for East Fife. You would not think I would find one over 160 miles away in Lossiemouth but that is what happened. I was there one July weekend to speak at the Baptist Church, led by our Lossiemouth chaplain at the time, Rae MacKenzie. We were walking along the road on our way to the Coasters' team bus to go to Lossie's away game against Rothes, so that I could meet their new chairman there. As we were chatting, Rae heard someone calling his name. He looked behind him and there was a man called Alexander Ritchie who had previously led the United Free Church in Lossiemouth. He happened to be there that weekend on holiday. I instantly took to Alexander and, when I asked where he was now ministering, I was delighted to hear him say he was based in Burntisland, only 14 miles from where East Fife play, in Methil. It turned out he was very interested in the chaplaincy role and I was delighted to introduce him to one of the directors John Donaldson a few months later. John was convinced he had met him somewhere before, and then it clicked. Alex had conducted John's son's wedding – you've guessed it, in Lossiemouth. An instant connection was made.

Another good piece of transfer business came in the form of the East Fife chaplain who I had replaced with Alexander. Richard Baxter had moved from Fife all the way to Fort William, at the very time when I had to replace their chaplain. What was even better was that, to begin with, Richard continued to wear his East Fife club tie to Fort William games, as their colours were exactly the same – gold and black. That is probably where the similarities ended for Richard as he had to wait for 73 games and 840 days before he witnessed a Fort William victory – no one could ever accuse him of being a glory hunter. Maybe he had not been praying hard enough…. But I think we have covered that one.

Going back to Lossiemouth – I hope you are still following me – having done a great job there, their chaplain, Rae MacKenzie dropped a bombshell by telling me he was moving to Dunfermline. However, it turned out well for the Fife club, because their chaplain was moving away to Ireland the same month as Rae was moving down. So, a seamless transition there, it just gave me a bit of a headache trying to replace him in Lossiemouth!

There have been a few transfers over the years and therein lies another big challenge for me. I am now used to that sinking feeling in my stomach when I receive a call from one our chaplains to tell me they are moving on. At the time of writing, we have 115 football club chaplains. Even if all of those chaplains were able to stay at their respective clubs for 10 years, this means I would have to replace about 11 chaplains every year. So the challenge is not only introducing chaplaincy to new clubs but also maintaining the service at our existing clubs.

172

CONFESSIONS OF A FOOTBALL CHAPLAIN

If someone has done a great job, I will seek to open up another opportunity for them. David Barrie became chaplain at Stirling Albion in 1998, the same year as I started at Thistle. When he moved to Pitlochry, we both knew it was not feasible for him to continue with the Binos. However, it would have been very sad to lose David to football chaplaincy because his excellent reputation is one of the reasons Sports Chaplaincy Scotland grew so much. At that time, I was beginning to make connections with St Johnstone and, since Perth is not that far from Pitlochry, I managed to appoint David at the Saints. He has been doing a grand job there since 2013, even becoming the Sports Chaplaincy Scotland "media darling" – appearing on Sky Sports News and in various newspapers.

Another of our chaplains, Graham Crawford, was at Elgin City, which was handy because his wife Jane was also the club doctor – a good partnership. However, Graham made the move to Perth. David Barrie was already at St Johnstone and so, since that was the only Senior club in the area, it meant that I was going to lose Graham's services. However, Jeanfield Swifts became one of a number of East Region Junior clubs that transferred over to the East of Scotland League. I had a ready-made and experienced chaplain for them!

I have found that one of the most fruitful ways of finding chaplains is being asked to speak at a church event on the subject of sports chaplaincy. On one occasion, I was asked to speak at such a service at the church of our Arbroath chaplain at that time, Martin Fair. The week before I was due to speak, Martin told me that there was a slight change of plans and that he would be conducting a baby's baptism at the service. There would be quite a few guests, most of whom would not normally come to church. I love these opportunities to share about Jesus with people who are completely unconnected to church. After explaining about chaplaincy in football, I said in the passing, "I know we're in Arbroath, but since we're quite close to Forfar, I thought I'd put it out there this morning that I'm looking for a female chaplain for Forfar Farmington who play in the Women's Premier League. If anyone here is interested to find out more, see me at the end of the service." To my surprise, as soon as we were finished, a young woman who, on her own admission, was not a Christian and did not normally connect with a church, marched up to me and said, "I think my mum would be brilliant at that!" I did not know what to think – normally church leaders recommend people to me, not someone's daughter. However, I felt it would only be mannerly to meet the young woman's mum. What a great recommendation this turned out to be! Susan Forbes has been a fantastic chaplain at Forfar Farmington, doubling up as the team nutritionist, a subject she teaches at the Academy there.

One of the most challenging appointments I have had to make was for Edusport Academy FC, now Caledonian Braves, who currently play in the Lowland League. The concept behind Edusport Academy was to provide an opportunity for young French players who had come out of the country's football academy system but had not been signed by a professional club. The deal was that they would learn English, while playing semi-professionally, and put themselves in a shop window for football scouts to see them. Hopefully they would then get their breakthrough into the professional game. When Edusport Academy were first admitted to the Lowland League, all of their players were French-speaking and a number of them spoke Arabic too, because they were of North African descent. It was going to be a challenge finding a chaplain for them. He would need to speak fluent French, and preferably Arabic too. He would also need to have an idea about French and North African culture. What a tall order!

I phoned up a friend who was well-connected and he shocked me by saying, "Mark, there's someone right under your very nose! Ross Hamilton, one of the guitarists in your church worship band!" Of course! Ross's dad, Grant, had previously worked as a social worker in Tunisia. In preparation for working in North Africa, he had to study in Paris, which meant moving his family over there. This had meant that Ross had gone to school in Paris and, as he was a talented footballer, he played in the youth system there too. Then, when Grant moved to Tunisia, Ross had to go too, thus having to learn Arabic. The only aspect of his time there that Ross enjoyed was playing football and developing his guitar skills. Looking back, he is very thankful for this life experience, as he became excellent at both. When Ross came back to Scotland, he was a very promising pro-youth player on Clyde's books. Sadly, a back injury destroyed his aspirations of making it as a professional player but even that, along with everything else in his background, made him the perfect chaplain for Edusport Academy. He has even been able to do some translation work for the manager.

Another reason why I should have known about Ross's availability was because his dad was already one of our chaplains – at Queen of the South. At the time of his appointment, Grant was the pastor of a Baptist Church in Cumbernauld. What on earth was I thinking, appointing him to the Dumfries club when he lived 80 miles away from the club? Well, at that time the club trained at Broadwood Stadium in Cumbernauld, because most of their players lived in Scotland's central belt. And that was within walking distance of Grant's house. What was even better was that Grant was originally from Dumfries and was a season ticket holder for the Doonhamers. So he did not need any encouragement to attend the home games at Palmerston as he was a frequent attender anyway. While Grant had been a dream appointment at Queen of the South, I did have to warn him of the big shoes he had to fill there.

Billy Kelly had been the first chaplain at Queens, and his tablet-making skills were legendary. For the non-Scottish reader, I am not referring to a mobile computer device. In Scotland, tablet is confectionary, usually made from sugar, condensed milk, and butter. Eventually, the management team of Jim McIntyre and Billy Dodds banned the chaplain from bringing any more of his sugary delights in for the players, as they were concerned about their limited nutritional value. However, they obviously did not want to offend him, so they continued to allow him to bring in his delicious tablet but just for them... Billy emigrated to Australia and sadly his tablet recipe went with him. Back to Grant, he has recently moved to Dumbarton, and yes, you've guessed right, I transferred him so that he is now chaplain to the Sons!

CONFESSIONS OF A FOOTBALL CHAPLAIN

This is what the process of appointing a chaplain looks like. First of all, a person will be recommended to me by someone who I know understands the personality, skillsets, experience and pastoral gifts that are necessary to be a football chaplain.

I will then have an informal chat with the prospective chaplain. It's actually an informal interview, but they don't realise that, or at least they didn't before reading this! I can usually make a fairly accurate judgement call within 20 seconds as to whether they are suitable – that is usually how long they have to connect to people they meet in a dressing room setting. In football culture, first impressions are vitally important, so if someone is painfully shy it simply will not work. Chaplains have to be relationally proactive – they need to be able to approach others with confidence rather than expecting people to come and build a relationship with them.

The next stage is that they have to fill out an "expression of interest form" on the Sports Chaplaincy UK website, in which they tell us about their motives for getting involved in chaplaincy. They have to include two referees – not the ones with whistles – so we can check up on their characters.

All going well, they will be invited to a training day for new chaplains at Hampden Park, usually in the SPFL boardroom. The full day's training gives them an understanding of how chaplaincy has developed in Scottish football, what particular and unique pressures are faced by people involved within the game, many practical pointers as to how they can best serve their respective clubs, information about safeguarding, and how to climb the acceptance ladder at a club. The training day also enables me to see how the candidates relate to others in a group setting.

At the end of the training day, I make an assessment on each person. If I feel they would be a good fit, the next stage is usually for the prospective chaplain and I to meet with the club chairman. If that goes well, we will meet with the club manager and coaching staff. If everyone is happy to proceed, we normally agree on a six month probationary period. On the rare occasion that it does not work out for any reason, it means that the club and the chaplain are not obliged to continue working with each other.

I will often introduce the chaplain to the squad, and explain the role, along the following lines: "I know that some of you night be thinking, 'What's this? The God squad coming into the dressing room?' Just to clarify, this isn't a religious role. The chaplain hasn't come here to ram the Bible down your throat. He's simply here to help, support and encourage you in any way he can. He's here to give you pastoral support in your mental, emotional and spiritual wellbeing. We are available to people of all faiths and individual beliefs. If you've got any struggles with life off the pitch he's someone you can talk to in complete confidence. He won't go telling the manager or anyone else. The only time he can't keep something confidential is if you indicate you're about to seriously harm yourself or someone else – apart from that it's between him and you. I know for some of you this might seem a little weird but give it time. As you get to know your chaplain and like and trust him, you'll find him a great asset. He may only ever be your friend but, for some of you, he might be a massive help – so make use of him."

This introduction was particularly important in the early days when chaplaincy was quite new in Scottish football. However, it's perhaps not so necessary now, as most players will be aware of what the chaplain can offer in the same way as they are aware of what the doctor and physiotherapist are there for.

My most memorable introduction of a chaplain took place at Edinburgh University FC, one of the founder members of the Lowland League and the first club from that division to have a chaplain appointed. This was no ordinary football dressing room. Football has long been the domain of the working classes in Scotland and it's probably fair to say that we don't have a proliferation of professional footballers who would consider themselves to be academic.

Edinburgh University FC was different because all of these players were students or alumni, so I had to take that into consideration when thinking of an appropriate chaplain for them. I knew a young American pastor from New Jersey, now working in Edinburgh, called Dave Goldschmidt. He was very warm and personable. The only slight potential issue was that he was clueless about football – or soccer in his case. As long as he did not mention that to the group I felt we would be fine – he would pick it up in time. I usually take a maximum of five minutes to explain to a dressing room of players what chaplaincy entails and the chaplain may take a further two minutes to introduce himself.

179

Not in Dave's case – he spent the next 20 minutes talking about how he felt he could help them as a chaplain, using a box of sweeties to deliver an object lesson. Worse still, he admitted he did not know the first thing about football, but was really into cage fighting. I was dying on the inside! Seriously, my back was wet with sweat, I was so embarrassed. Inside my head I am screaming, "Mate, stop, just stop, you're killing me! You can't speak to a group of players for that length of time and expect to keep their attention." Then I looked up and saw that the guys were absolutely loving this American dude. He was relating brilliantly to them. They really took to Dave, and at the end of the season, he put on a big barbeque and a PlayStation FIFA competition for them. I am not sure how much his football knowledge has improved but the guys think the world of him regardless.

Another of our American chaplains is Brandon Newman, who started off at the Coatbridge club, Albion Rovers. This must have been out of his comfort zone because he was from Dallas, Texas and he was more familiar with a basketball court than with a football pitch. Notwithstanding, he threw himself into the role of a football chaplain. They loved him there, even though he was an easy target for mickey taking, given his limited experience in Scottish footballing culture. He used to travel to training with two players. On one journey they told him about one of their teammates who they were really concerned about. This player had "big problems" and needed a chat with Brandon but they told him the lad was too shy to approach the chaplain.

Brandon sensitively approached the player at training to subtly find out how he was doing, reminding him that he was always available if the player needed him. The young man expressed his gratitude to Brandon, albeit looking at him with a rather mystified look on his face. That was until both of them noticed the two teammates who had set up "the appointment" knotting themselves laughing! I can assure you that this and other similar incidents have nothing to do with the fact that Brandon moved on from football to become the first chaplain at Scotland's only professional basketball club, Glasgow Rocks.

CHAPTER 15

WHAT DOES A CHAPLAIN DO?

If you were to ask Tommy Taylor, the club photographer at Partick Thistle, what a chaplain does, he would probably tell you that he uses his special powers to make it rain for 90 minutes right from kick-off. In fact, Tommy even called me the Rain Man, because he was convinced that every time I came to Firhill, regardless of the weather prior to my arrival or what the forecast was, it always pelted down. It's not true of course, but I always have a right laugh when I'm sitting in the stand and poor Tommy is getting drenched as he sits pitch-side trying to take photos.

I was speaking to a director of a club a few years ago at a match. He said that prior to the appointment of their chaplain, he would never have seen the need of having one. I suppose you cannot miss what you have never had! Now, he would place the same importance on having a chaplain as he would on having a doctor and a physiotherapist. The latter have obvious roles in a football club, usually related to helping a player recover from physical injury. It's a bit different for the chaplain. We are there to give pastoral support in the areas of mental, emotional and spiritual wellbeing. However, for this to happen, people at the football club need to know you, like you, understand your role and trust you. This does not happen overnight. Sometimes chaplains are not quite sure what to do during the period of time that it takes to build those relationships of trust.

CONFESSIONS OF A FOOTBALL CHAPLAIN

Someone once used the expression "loitering with intent" to describe what chaplains do. We help out in practical ways so that, if pastoral needs arise, we have already built up such a good relationship that people will come to us. To some, the chaplain may never be anything other than a friend, but if he is a life-saver to just one person, it's worth it.

Part of my role as Scottish Director for Sports Chaplaincy UK is ensuring quality control. So when I get a chance to meet a manager I always ask him how his chaplain is doing. I happened to bump in to one manager who was attending a game because his team were not playing that Saturday. Of course, I asked how his chaplain was doing and I was utterly shocked when he told me he was not even aware that they *had* a club chaplain! I was quite angry, because the chaplain had led me to believe that he was there every week at training and at home match days. Why would he have lied to me about that?

I got in touch with the chaplain to tell him what the manager had said but he too was shocked. He insisted that he had been at training just about every Thursday night and always said hello to the manager and chatted to the players. This required further investigation. The upshot was that the chaplain had never officially introduced himself or explained what he did when the manager was appointed at the club. Consequently, the manager just thought he was this nice, friendly supporter who rocked up to training every Thursday night to say hello!

In saying that, I have my own confession to make in this area. As mentioned before, I trained with Partick Thistle every Friday morning and this went on for nine seasons. We had a chiropodist, called Kate, who also hosted some of the players in her home. I always said hello to Kate before going off to train, but I did not really get into much conversation beyond everyday chit-chat. After a couple of years, she said to John Lambie, "John, there's a player I see every Friday when I'm in doing the players' feet but he never seems to get a game on Saturday. Poor lad, God's obviously not on his side." John replied, "Kate, of course God's on his side, he's the club ****** chaplain!" Therein lies an important lesson to all chaplains – never assume that people know who you are simply because they see you around the club. It is very important to introduce yourself to everyone and explain what you are there for, especially when there are changes of personnel at the club.

I have found that there is usually someone at the club who you would identify as "the gatekeeper". This person does not necessarily have any church connection but simply "gets you", understands why you are there and appreciates the value of your role. It can be the club secretary, the physiotherapist, kit man - anyone who genuinely cares for the wellbeing of everyone there and is a person of influence.

In my case at Partick Thistle, the person who helped me the most to settle in, and make me feel involved at the club, was the captain, Danny Lennon. Danny had previously played at Raith Rovers and they had been one of the very few Scottish clubs at that time that had a chaplain – Neil MacMillan. Danny got on very well with Neil and that must have helped us make an instant connection when he came to Firhill. Danny went to great lengths to make me feel an integral part of the club,

184

including making sure I was involved in all the social events. I do not have the words to express how grateful I am to him because I really did feel like a fish out of water at times, way out of my depth – I think that's what you call a mixed metaphor!

So what does a chaplain actually do then? To sum up, we will do anything we can to bring practical or pastoral support where it is needed. People with no previous experience of a good chaplain might well be excused for being cynical, especially if they have no belief in God. Bill Sharp was chaplain to East Stirlingshire, who currently play in the Lowland League. He told me of the time when he had just started at the club and was in conversation with Tadek Kopszywa, their media guru and match secretary. Tad had told Bill straight that he was an atheist and did not believe in God. Bill reassured him and reminded him that he was happy to serve those of all faiths and individual beliefs – including those who believe there is no God! He coined a phrase that his role was "faith-based but not faith-biased".

Towards the end of a training session, one of the players approached Bill and asked if he could talk with him and Tad. He began to share a difficult situation that he was in. Bill spoke with him and pointed him in the direction of a support organisation. When the lad had left, Tad turned to Bill and said, "Thank God you are here, I don't know what I would have done there!" I can see the headlines now – "Atheist thanks God for Chaplain's Arrival!"

Bill tells of how he noticed that, heading into the winter, the players were coming into training straight from work. The weather was terrible and the cold nights meant the players simply trained, showered and went home. So he decided to buy them a soup kettle for Christmas. On a freezing cold and wet December night, when they came back in to the dressing room, they were welcomed with a warm bowl of chicken rice soup with some crusty bread and butter. After training that night, the players and management team tucked in and sat for about an hour chatting.

This became a feature of every session. Soon the manager, players and backroom staff took turns to make soup and this developed into creating more elaborate dishes. Obviously, being a competitive bunch, a league table was started. Apparently the Gaffer's hot dogs took him to top spot.

Even though we attend training sessions to get to know everyone, much of our good work is done away from the ground and sometimes at the most awkward of times. Our chaplain at Dundee United, Andy Burns, also runs an organisation called Rock Street Chaplains. It is very similar to another organisation called Street Pastors, with which you may be more familiar. They offer practical pastoral support to people who go out clubbing and find themselves in vulnerable situations due to their overindulgence in alcohol. These chaplains work tremendously well with the police and ambulance crews in keeping people safe. Andy has been awarded an MBE because of his work in Dundee.

CONFESSIONS OF A FOOTBALL CHAPLAIN

One evening, in his role as a nightclub chaplain, Andy was approached by one of the door staff of a particular establishment in Dundee. He was informed that some of the United development squad were in the VIP lounge, and some were a little the worse for wear. Andy managed to get three of them into his car to take them back to their lodgings. All was going well until one of the lads said he was going to be sick. Before Andy could stop the car, the inevitable happened. He thought he heard someone crying out, "Hughie!" To be fair, the lad had managed to find a basket in the back of the car in which to empty the contents of his stomach. The only downside to this was that it was a basket with freshly washed and laundered clothes that Andy was supposed to be taking back to his house. The car was malodorous for days afterwards. Let's just say Andy had to make a return trip to the launderette to stay in the good books with his wife!

A number of years ago, I met a former United player, who positively raved about Andy. "Aw, we had the best chaplain for sure", he said, "I had been banned from most night clubs in Dundee so I asked our Rev if he could speak with the manager of Fat Sam's and get me in there. Top man managed to get me and all my mates in – and for free too..." Not usually one of the services Sports Chaplaincy Scotland provides, but it was certainly appreciated by this player!

Another unique role was carried out by James Stout, chaplain at Whitehill Welfare. The groundsman was struggling with issues regarding the club's pitch, but one of the main problems was that rabbits were chewing the goal nets, digging up the ground and causing general mayhem.

James suggested that he could help by taking out the rabbits – and I don't mean taking them out to dinner, I mean taking them out in the American fashion – with a gun! Well, James is a bit of a crack shot and he managed to take six of them out! When I posted this story on our Scottish football chaplains' Facebook page, only visible to our chaplains for reasons of confidentiality, he received a great response, including a picture of Bugs Bunny and Elmer Fudd. So, we have now nicknamed James, "Elmer". We decided to drop his surname on account of the fact that Fudd is not a name you really want to be called if you are from Scotland – if you don't understand then google it!

There are a number of practical things our chaplains have done to help out their clubs. Duncan Strathdee, our chaplain at Stirling Albion, earned his bus driving licence so that he could save his club money by driving the team bus to games. Jon Bergen at Brechin City video recorded the games and provided a copy for the manager by Monday morning. Alex Morrison at Huntly and Thomas Urquhart at Clachnacuddin take in ticket money at the turnstiles. Rob Wilson at Vale of Leithen and Don Currie at Saltcoats Victoria took on the role of club secretary, which is purely an administrative role with no decision-making capacity. Several of our chaplains have been appointed as wellbeing officers at their respective clubs.

In terms of training nights, most of us act as ball boys/girls. Some of us will get involved in the running and passing drills, though very few will take any more part than that.

CONFESSIONS OF A FOOTBALL CHAPLAIN

For months, the head coach of Spartans Women had been joking about getting one of their chaplains, Mel Crolla, more involved in training. She encouraged her to have a kick about with the girls at the beginning of the session while they were gathering together. However, Mel felt sorry for the goalkeepers who train by themselves most of the night, so she thought she would keep them company and help out. On one occasion, she could see the two goalkeepers were trying to sort out a training session. Only one of them was able to feed the ball to the other goalkeeper. Using her initiative, she offered to help. The exact words that came out of her mouth were, "I'm sure I can manage to throw a ball". Well, it turns out she could not throw a ball very accurately, though she was a dab hand at receiving it back, square in the face! She has gone back to loitering with intent, at a distance....

While most of what we do is good fun, we are not having a jolly. There is a purpose behind these relationship-building exercises. When crisis comes, if people already know us, like us, understand our role and trust us, then there is more likelihood that they will turn to us.

CHAPTER 16

THE OBJECTIVITY OF THE CHAPLAIN

I am often asked if it is beneficial for the chaplain to be a supporter of the club.   There is no correct answer to that, as there can be pros and cons on both sides of the argument. If you are a supporter, you are likely to be very committed to your club and you will be willing to go the second mile in your service. Having said that, I have found that when someone becomes a club chaplain this happens anyway. The club grabs your heart and any other previous allegiances begin to wane as you wholeheartedly get behind your new team.

Off the top of my head, I can think of five chaplains who would ordinarily support Celtic, Rangers, Aberdeen, Hearts and Hibernian respectively. However, I can confidently say that they would support the clubs they are now chaplain of, if they were to play their original favourites. If you are not a supporter of the club before you become their chaplain, you may be better equipped to bring an emotional equilibrium to the club. Having said that, although our role is not performance-related, it is surely legitimate to grieve when the livelihoods of people are affected by the results on the park.

When I became chaplain at Partick Thistle, the biggest change for me was that, whereas I had been a supporter of the club, I changed into a supporter of the people *working at* the club. There is a big difference.

CONFESSIONS OF A FOOTBALL CHAPLAIN

In the past I would have been one of those people who would not have really bothered who was wearing red and yellow, as long as they played well and we won. Don't get me wrong – as chaplain, you want the team to win but for different reasons. You know that a victory means a win bonus for someone who is now a friend. It means it is safe for him to look at social media. It means an enjoyable weekend for his partner and family. It means the manager's job is safe for at least another week. It means the chairman can safely walk the streets without being verbally abused or physically threatened. It means a little more job security for all the administration staff and others in the background of the club. So, whilst at Thistle I certainly felt the impact of a defeat, it was because I knew the effect that such a result would have on many others. I would have to admit that I did let disappointments affect me much more than they should have, albeit I was able to get over them fairly quickly.

In August 2015, Thistle were beating Kilmarnock 2-1, going into the closing stages of the game. I was savouring a victory. However, Kris Boyd scored with five minutes to go and we drew the match 2-2. It felt like a loss, we had certainly dropped two points. I sat with my head in my hands, rocking back and forth, nearly in tears of frustration – not as a supporter, but utterly gutted for these boys. As the families of the players were leaving their seats, they were coming up to me to put their arm around me to comfort me. My wife turned to me and said, "Mark you're the chaplain, you're supposed to be giving comfort to everyone else and it's you who's needing a chaplain! Get a grip!" Fair comment.

CONFESSIONS OF A FOOTBALL CHAPLAIN

It was probably just as well that I came in to Firhill on a Friday, as that gave me nearly a week to recover from the disappointment of a poor result. However, I would not want to give you the impression that poor form adversely affected my attitude towards the players. Far from it, I wanted to cheer everyone up. In fact, one player turned to me on a gloomy Friday morning, in the midst of a poor run of results, and asked, "Rev, how come you're always ******* smiling?!" I didn't have the heart to reply that it certainly wasn't because of his recent performances….

There have been occasions when I have felt it was not appropriate for a supporter of the club to be appointed as chaplain. When Craig Brown became manager of Aberdeen, I met with him to discuss the possibility of chaplaincy at Pittodrie. Craig was very enthusiastic about the prospect, having had a great chaplain in Chris Nelson, when he managed Preston North End in England. My favourite story Craig tells is of the time when one of his players was subject to angry complaints from his neighbours. They were claiming that the player's dog had been left outside in his garden all week and it seemed to be very hungry and distressed as if it had been abandoned. Craig was aware that the player had gone home to Ireland for a week's break. Surely he would not have cruelly thrown his dog out of the house and allowed it to go without food? Craig phoned the player and asked him for an explanation. "I don't understand it Gaffer, sure I left my dog outside in his kennel, but I left him enough food to last him the week!" Craig called upon his chaplain, who was a well-liked local Vicar, to pour oil on this troubled water.

CONFESSIONS OF A FOOTBALL CHAPLAIN

Anyway, back to Aberdeen… I managed to source someone who I thought would be a great fit, but when I met with Craig again he had a dilemma because he had also been given another option. A local minister, who was a huge Dons fan, had turned up to watch a team training session and boldly approached Craig, asking for the opportunity to be chaplain. Immediately alarm bells were ringing with me. In fact, in the majority of cases that I have been made aware of, when someone has directly approached the club, particularly if it is a full-time professional club, and asked to be their chaplain, the person has been unsuitable. I would be concerned that they merely want to find out what is going on behind the scenes of the club, and bask in reflected glory if the team is doing well. I certainly could not have been accused of doing that at Thistle!

Whilst I will make recommendations of someone as a potential chaplain, I will always defer to the club in terms of the ultimate choice of candidate. After all, he is going to be *their* chaplain. However, I did express my concerns to Craig about this supporter. I was also very confident that my man was going to do a great job too. Craig went with my advice and he was very glad that he did. Barry Douglas has done a brilliant job at Aberdeen. I doubt if there will be anyone employed by the club who does not know him and the feedback that I have had from every department has been great.

One of the biggest dangers of a supporter becoming a chaplain is that there may be a temptation to get involved in the politics of the club, which is a big "no-no" for us.

Chaplains are told to keep their opinions to themselves on club affairs, but this can be quite a challenge if you have been used to expressing your views prior to your appointment. If you see someone being publicly misrepresented or treated unfairly, particularly if they have been a faithful servant of the club over many years, it is very difficult to keep your mouth shut. But we have to stay neutral.

The chaplain's place in a football club is unique in that we are there for absolutely everyone – the chairman, the board of directors, the manager, the coaching staff, the medical staff, the players, the kit men and the administration staff. We should be the one person at the club who *everyone* can trust and confide in. We have no axe to grind, no political power, and no decision-making capacity. This means that we need to be careful not to spend all of our time with one particular group at the club.

For example, when I was at Partick Thistle, I would make sure I spread myself as evenly as possible throughout the club. When I arrived first thing on Friday morning, I would go and have a cup of tea with the manager. Then I would pop into the physiotherapist's room to see him and also the players who would be arriving early in order to receive treatment. Then, I would be in the dressing room with the players and go off to training with them.

At lunch time I made sure that I sat at a different table every week. You often found that the senior players would sit at one table, the younger lads at another table and the coaching staff at another. On home match days I was looking after the families of players, so I did not have a chance to check in with the chairman and directors. However, they were kind enough to allow me to travel on the team bus to away matches. On the way to the game, I would sit next to them and also other background staff like the kit men. On the way back from games, where I sat depended on how the result had gone. If we had won, I was usually part of the players group banter, but if we had been defeated, I would sensitively decide whether I should quietly sit next to a player who needed a bit of encouragement or just sit in silence like everyone else. The manager was the one who usually set the tone for the whole bus. If he was in a foul mood, banter or even animated chatter, was not acceptable.

The one exception that I can remember was returning from Inverness after a 3-0 defeat. John Lambie was so happy, you would have thought that we had *won* 3-0. I could not help but ask him – why the cheery disposition? Well, we had already won the title and were guaranteed promotion to the Premier League so the result did not have any bearing on our position. However, the reason he was delighted was because he did not have to hand out win bonuses to the players that week – so he had more money for his budget the following season. Now that is what I call an objective perspective!

So many people have said to me, "Why do footballers need a chaplain? They must be living the dream, making loads of easy money, enjoying themselves chasing a ball around a park every week." These people do not understand the reality of life as a footballer in Scotland. Sure, there are a few players at the top end who make good money out of the game, but the vast majority will never earn enough to provide themselves with a "nest egg" for the future. Not only that, squads are getting smaller, the football scrap heap is getting bigger and contracts are getting shorter.

At this juncture I am going insert a written piece given to me by a friend who is a well-known professional player. I am going to remove his name and certain details that may make it obvious who he is, in order to protect his anonymity. He entitled the piece, *"Scared"* and he inserts lyrics from the song *"Salem's Interlude"* by Khalid.

> *PLAY - "engage in activity for enjoyment and recreation rather than a serious or practical purpose"*
>
> *I LOVE "playing" football. Football is all I know and all I've ever really been "good" at. But the problem is I don't "play" football, I'm in the industry that is football. Where is the enjoyment in sitting in the changing room before a game petrified as to what could happen in the next few hours?*
>
> *I don't want to let myself down, my teammates, my family or friends that have come to watch - all expecting me to do well. But I can't turn round to a teammate and say, "I'm scared about going out here." No, I sit there and do what everyone knows I'm good at, PRETENDING I'M NOT BOTHERED. And I almost convince myself I'm not.*
>
> *When I'm having a bad game people will say you just didn't look interested. But deep down it's killing me inside, and I look like I'm not trying but I'm trying even harder. I feel physically embarrassed.*

I'm embarrassed because I know I'm better than most players on a football pitch at this level but for some reason I can't bring myself to be better than them and it's all in my own head because I know I'm petrified to let anyone down. I scored 26 goals in a season for ****** and emotionally that was the worst season I had. I hated it. At the end of that season I broke down crying on the side of the road on my way home for easily 15 minutes and I was thinking what the **** is wrong with me? I've just had the best season of my life and I hate it!

The problem for me is that with all the highs comes a horrible feeling of anxiety, anxious of people's expectations and then those I put on myself. People say when you score it gives you confidence and I understand what they're saying because it does, but the overwhelming emotion for me is anxiety. I just feel it's even more pressure and I just don't like it really but that's just the territory I'm in I guess.

> *Salem's Interlude - Khalid*

> *"I'm fearful of failure*
> *I'm fearful of being embarrassed*
> *Things like that, I think hinder me from doing the best*
> *that I can sometimes*
> *But I think that if I learn to be less fearful*
> *I would get further*
> *I feel like I'm not always in the correct direction*
> *Even though I know I'm on the right path"*

CONFESSIONS OF A FOOTBALL CHAPLAIN

I think the biggest reason I get so scared at times is because football is all I've known for so long, I've seen so many people better than me fall away and not be able to play anymore and it scares me to think everything that comes with "playing" football can be taken away from you at any time and that I could be left with nothing, especially now I have a son to take care of in the world as well.

*I know 1000000% I am incredibly fortunate to be able to go and do what I do for a living every single day. In this country it's thousands of kids' dreams to grow up and be a footballer. I can honestly say from a young age it was never mine, I remember going to matches [at various well-known football clubs] and even at that age the environments were toxic. I was 9-13, competing with entitled kids who thought they were the ******* because they played for an academy. I'd love to see how many of them kids made it.*

*I've always tried to keep myself grounded because from a young age I've never enjoyed that environment that comes with football, the "I'm better than you" environment, the "let's talk about him in this corner behind his back" environment. Don't get me wrong, I've been in the game for 10 years and I've definitely been dragged into it at times. But football as a whole is a toxic, acidic environment and every single person is in it for themselves. So when I'm sitting in the changing room, ******** myself before a game, thinking about all the people I'm going to let down, what gives me the confidence to turn to my left and say "Listen mate, I'm feeling nervous about going out here"? None! I have zero confidence in any of them.*

198

CONFESSIONS OF A FOOTBALL CHAPLAIN

I've been in the game for 10 years now, I can honestly say there are three people I would call friends. A lot of people I'd stop and say hello to, get a night out with, but there are only three of those people I would even consider sending this to. In fact I'd only send it to one of them. That says a lot about an industry where you meet hundreds of people in your short career.

I've been meaning to do this for months now, to share this, but to be honest I've been scared to actually put these words into reality and show anyone how I feel because it's embarrassing for me to feel this way and to share it but I suppose the only way to combat it is to get it out there. So this is just a kid scared to fail and let people down I guess.

I find these words incredibly revealing and moving. The role of a chaplain is to see past the player and see the person. Football supporters are often only interested in players in terms of how they perform and what they achieve on the park. It seems to me that footballers are dehumanised by some fans. That player is simply the No. 9, somebody wearing *their* team colours. If they play well, score and win they are idolised. However, if they don't meet the expectations of supporters they can be vilified. Some of what I have heard supporters shout at players has horrified me. Stewards should be empowered to take firm action against people like this. In any other context, these abusive fans would be arrested for breach of the peace or for threatening violent behaviour. There are signs around football grounds warning that foul and abusive language will not be tolerated – and yet it is. Football grounds seem to have a law of their own.

If only fans would realise that they are actually defeating their objective in being at the match – to support the team. Believe me, when players hear "fans" hurling abuse at them – it hurts! It knocks their confidence. It demoralises, discourages and ultimately demotivates them. By all means, express your frustration under your breath, but for the sake of your team, only shout if you have something positive to contribute.

And it's not just the players who get it on the neck from fans. I have already written about the abuse managers can receive. I have also seen chairmen being verbally and even physically abused by fans. Why should they have to put up with that? Also, before you hurl abuse at a player, manager or chairman, just remember he is someone's son, someone's partner – would you like similar abuse to be hurled at you or any of your family members?

Fans may also not realise the impact of poor results on everyone working in the background at the club, particularly in the administration department. It can lead to very low morale and anxiety because they know that their jobs are on the line should the club be relegated to a lower tier.

Even at a national level there are similar pressures on non-playing staff. I remember a friend who had a leading role in the Scottish FA commercial sponsoring department, who told me of a situation that illustrates this. The Scotland Men's team had been defeated in a European Championship qualifying match in Eastern Europe and this now meant it was very unlikely that they would reach the finals.

On the flight back home, my friend sat with a blanket over her head, trying not to cry. This was because she knew how difficult it was going to be to procure sponsorship for forthcoming games, which were now effectively meaningless.

I often hear people say, "Football is all about opinions." Yet, I have heard players say that they have not felt their opinions have been valued and listened to. The area of listening is such an important part of a chaplain's role. I would say that, historically, there used to be more trust between teammates but because contracts are now generally much shorter, that player who you confide in as a friend today, could become your opponent next season. The chaplain is unique in that their role is not directly performance-related. That said, they could be a bridge between people at a football club.

At Partick Thistle, we signed a player who had played at a higher level but he just did not seem to be cutting it with us. The manager at the time, John Lambie, was not happy. "That was some ******* signing I made with him! He hasn't kicked his **** since he's come here." That is me editing it by the way. I could see myself that the player was struggling, so I drew alongside him and asked if he was happy at the club. "Firhill is fine Rev, it's my personal life that's a nightmare just now. I've been an idiot but my wife won't forgive me and I just can't focus on my game." We chatted further and I gave him some advice, but then I also said, "Listen, can I advise you to go to the Gaffer and tell him about this? He won't judge you or reject you – he's far more understanding than a lot of people give him credit it for. You don't want him to think you're just not trying do you?" He took my advice and the manager gave him some time off to get his head sorted. When he came back, he was a different player and helped us achieve great success that season.

Another time a young player confided in me that he was really frustrated at Firhill. He simply could not see himself getting a breakthrough because the manager seemed to be sticking with the older, more experienced players. I could see that his frustration was really getting to him and that it was negatively affecting his attitude during training in a way that was not going to endear him to the manager. I was in the manager's office one day after training and asked him what he thought of the young player, "Oh he's a talent that boy, he'll play at a higher level than us one day. His chance is coming soon, he just needs to show a bit more hunger." Now, obviously confidentiality is a vital part of our role. However, I am a great believer in what I call "positive gossip." What I mean by that is, if I hear someone being praised by another person and I think they would get a lift from hearing about it, I will happily be a conduit of encouragement. So, I took the young lad aside and said to him, "The Gaffer really rates you! I was talking to him and he was telling me that he thinks that you're a great talent, that you'll play at a higher level and your chance is coming soon. But listen son, see the way you're training, you've got a big chip on your shoulder that's slowing you down – get rid of it and get a smile on your face so that when your time comes you're ready to grasp the opportunity and make the most of it. Get into a positive frame of mind!" He took my advice, was selected, scored on his debut and yes, he went on to play at a higher level.

On another occasion we had a situation where we had signed a player but, after a few games in which he had made mistakes, you could see the confidence draining from him. The inevitable happened – he was dropped. That obviously did not help his confidence, nor was he very happy, and this affected the atmosphere of the dressing room. The manager felt that the player's attitude and demeanour were not helpful to the rest of the first-team players and so he made him train with the younger players. This is a very familiar story.

This exacerbated the player's unhappiness, until it got to the stage where he wanted to leave the club. That suited the manager because the player was no longer in his plans. The general manager also realised that it would be better for all concerned if the player moved on. There was a problem though. The player wanted his contract paid up. However, the club needed the money that was being paid to him to be freed up so they could sign someone to replace him. All sides took an entrenched position and nobody was happy. I looked at the situation objectively. The player's continuation at the club was not doing anyone any good. It was no good to the player because he was not going to be selected and he was quickly going to be forgotten as a footballer. It was not going to look good on his CV and he was only going to become increasingly unhappy and demoralised. It was no good to the manager because of the negativity emanating from this situation and he was adamant that the player would not feature in the first team again. The general manager was caught in the middle, but there was now a breakdown in communication.

CONFESSIONS OF A FOOTBALL CHAPLAIN

Because all concerned trusted me, I felt I was in the strongest position to act as a mediator as I only wanted what was best for everyone. Thankfully, we managed to come to an agreement. Part of the player's contract was paid up to him and the club were able to bring someone in to replace him in the next transfer window. If I ever thought a player was been treated unjustly, I would probably encourage them to go to PFA Scotland, who act on their behalf. A chaplain cannot take sides in disputes because of our neutrality.

This type of situation illustrates why it is important that a chaplain is placed by Sports Chaplaincy Scotland and not by the chairman of a football club. I personally think such a scenario would hinder a relationship of trust between the chaplain and management. It would only be natural for the manager to suspect that the chaplain was sent by the chairman to spy on him.

We all need someone to offload to during times of frustration, in the knowledge that it will not go anywhere. The chaplain listens to people because he is passionate about them and wants their views and feelings to be valued. He should do so without judging them, gossiping about them or rejecting them. A chaplain will be conscious of only offering his view if asked and will keep whatever is said in confidence – unless someone indicates they are going to seriously harm themselves or someone else. In that case, the chaplain is legally bound to address the matter according to the club's safeguarding policies. Apart from that, the chaplain could be the one person in the club who everyone can confide in.

It might also be a good time to reiterate that the chaplain is not there to give advice on selection, tactics or any other footballing matters, we leave the manager to get on with that. I would be horrified if I ever heard that a chaplain went into the manager's office and said, "Gaffer, I was praying last night and the Lord spoke to me and told me to pass on a message to you: ditch that 4-4-2 formation and go 4-1-4-1. Oh, and while you're at it, you should bring the number 14 back into the first team." You can safely assume that such a chaplain would be reprimanded or even removed!

CHAPTER 17

WE DON'T DO DEATH REV

"We don't do death, Rev." This was said by the manager of a football club to a newly appointed chaplain. What he meant was that he was relieved that there was someone in place who could support everyone at the club who had been affected by the recent death of a staff member. Many of our chaplains have good experience in supporting and counselling the bereaved, helping people through the grieving process.

In 2015, Heart of Midlothian opened up the "Forever In Our Hearts Memorial Garden" on the site of the famous Tynecastle Shed at the corner of the Wheatfield and Roseburn Stands. It was the brainchild of their chief operating officer at the time, Scott Gardiner, after he had seen something similar at Manchester City.

The centrepiece is a beautiful bronze and steel sculpture of the club's iconic crest with a bronze football in the centre that people are encouraged to touch in order to feel connected with the club. There is also a custom-built room for quiet reflection. Supporters have the opportunity to honour a friend or loved one with a personalised engraved heart that proudly adorns the walls of the garden.

Their club chaplain, Andy Prime, conducts a simple monthly memorial service, and he is able to mingle with supporters and offer a listening ear to them as well. I attended one of these services and it was so moving to listen to different people tell me the story of the passing of their loved one, some in really tragic circumstances. Each person told me of how this opportunity to honour their loved one in the setting of Tynecastle was so cathartic to them. One woman there had bought a plaque for her deceased brother. She knew it would have meant to so much to him, even though she herself was a Hibernian supporter. If Andy is unavailable I usually step in for him. It's a fantastic service that the club offers to their supporters, and a good example of the commitment Ann Budge has to making their fans feel an intrinsic part of the Hearts family.

When Chic Charnley was on the coaching staff at Partick Thistle, he was told about a young Jags supporter, Ross, who was suffering with Ewing's Sarcoma, a vicious form of leukaemia. Chic was absolutely brilliant with Ross. He arranged trips to take him to Hampden, Ibrox and Parkhead. Of course, Chic also ensured that Ross and his dad got the best of treatment from his beloved Partick Thistle. This was where I came in. First of all, I was asked to look after Ross and his dad at matches at Firhill. We had a special place where we could take Ross's wheelchair so that he had a reasonable view of the game. Occasionally, if the result went our way, he was allowed into the changing room to join the celebrations with the players.

The horrendous form of bone cancer caused Ross's health to deteriorate rapidly. I got to know his family well during that time and I gave them pastoral visits. Aileen and I looked after the family's pet dog so they could go abroad on holiday. We did anything we could to enable them to have as much quality family time with Ross as possible. However, no matter how much you try and bring joy and comfort to people, nothing can make up for the pain of watching a young loved one slowly die in front of you. This is what Ross's family had to endure, not to speak of what the young boy was feeling, as he could feel life draining away from him. Even though we understood that he would eventually succumb to this horrible illness, it did not make it any less painful when he eventually died. No parent ever expects to attend the funeral of their children – it should be the other way round. I have been involved in many tragic situations like this but it never becomes any easier. I was honoured to be asked to conduct Ross's funeral.

As a minister, it is important to empathise with a family but, there comes a point when you have to park your own feelings, pull yourself together and be strong for them. I wanted to be able to pay tribute to Ross and to his family, who had remained so strong for him and supportive of him during his illness. Usually, I will go into the vestry or office before the service and, depending on the situation, have a good cry to try and release the raw emotions I am feeling, before going out to lead the service. However, as I was trying to gather my thoughts and hold myself together, Chic Charnley walked in. Now, remember Chic is known as one of the hardest men in the history of Scottish football, sent off more times than anyone else. He is a hard man from Possilpark – so you would think. Chic came into the vestry and burst into tears, sobbing uncontrollably, such was his grief for young Ross. He had grown so attached to this young lad and his family. This is a side to Chic that I have seen more than once, because he has a heart of compassion. I hugged him until he was able pull himself together, then we went into the main part of the crematorium. With an almighty struggle, I managed to hold back the tears during what was a very moving service.

The family had asked if we could have a memorial service back at Firhill and then for Ross's ashes to be scattered in the goalmouth area. Having the memorial service was no problem, but the club groundsman was not happy at the ashes being scattered in the penalty box, as they would potentially burn the grass and it was not in particularly good condition as it was. So, we agreed with the family that we would scatter Ross's ashes behind the goals. I conducted the memorial service and Chic carried out the scattering of the ashes, though not behind the goals, but exactly where Ross had wanted them – in the goalmouth area. I for one was not going to argue with Chic!

The largest ever attendance at a funeral I have conducted was in Kinlochbervie, in the Western Highlands. It was also probably one of the most difficult funerals I have ever had to conduct because it was for my good friend, Ally Macleod. I credit Ally with opening the door for me to pioneer chaplaincy in the Highland League.

As I mentioned in the chapter, 'For if you know the history...", Ally was assistant manager at Nairn County when he attended the UEFA A Licence coaching course at Largs in 2013. He had shared with me about how the club captain had suffered a personal tragedy during the season. The player's wife had sadly lost their baby, and Ally felt that having a club chaplain would have been a great support to the club during that time. As it was, a local church minister had a connection with the player, and he proved to be a significant help to him. It made sense for me to meet this minister and see if he would make a good football chaplain. Rev Steve Manders was a one-off. When I met him at Nairn train station, I thought he would be picking me up in his car. Except he did not have one. No, he had a bicycle. He had somehow managed to use his left hand to steer his bicycle and his right hand to steer a second bicycle, which was to be my mode of transport. As we cycled through the town, it seemed like he was the pastor of the whole community, let alone his church, as everybody warmly greeted him. This larger-than-life character was a great fit for the role and served at Nairn County until he moved to Edinburgh a number of years later.

During all this time Ally was battling the condition of Myelofibrosis. He continued with life as best as he could until in 2012, when his condition deteriorated. He was advised that a stem cell transplant was a possible cure. Ally was delighted that his brother, Lawrence, was a cell match. The treatment started in January 2014. Because he was being treated in Glasgow, I was able to go and visit him regularly, and we bonded over this time. The transplant was a difficult process, but through time, Ally came back to near normal health and quickly slipped back into his old life. However, in 2016, Ally received the devastating news that he had relapsed and would face another transplant at some point in the future. Even so, he seemed to be coping well, and I had the joy of conducting Ally and his fiancée Alanna's wedding in December 2017. However, in April of the following year, Ally had to go the Beatson Clinic in Glasgow to start treatment for his next transplant. Sadly, complications resulted in him being transferred to the Queen Elizabeth ICU.

Ally was a true fighter, and right up to the end he strongly fought to stay with us. His body was simply not strong enough for him to hold on. I found it really hard to accept that Ally had died, I had been so confident that he would pull through. When I was asked to conduct Ally's funeral, I wasn't too sure how I would be able to cope with the grief myself, let alone support his family.

There was such a mix of emotions. There were many laughs as I recounted stories about Ally, but understandably there was unspeakable sadness, frustration and anger. I wish I could have explained why this had happened. Although, while this is a horrible situation to go through, I would rather go through it *with* God's comfort, strength and peace than without it.

Life is fragile at the best of times. Ally's illness brought that reality into sharp focus. I still find it hard to take in that eight months after conducting his wedding, I had the responsibility of conducting his funeral. Alanna was expecting their baby when Ally passed away, which added to the sadness. Yet, this meant that Ally was able to leave a part of himself with us.

I have already mentioned conducting the funeral of my good friend John Lambie. While that was a sad occasion, John had lived a fairly full life. You will recall that he had given me strict instructions that he did not want dour hymns but lively, gospel music.

Thankfully, I was in a strong place to deliver. My wife and I had been associate pastors with Destiny Church, Glasgow. The church was replete with talented gospel singers and musicians. And so Pauline, backed by her husband Sam and another musician, Dade, belted out "Oh Happy Day" – Sister Act style! Then she sang the ballad, "Because He Lives I Can Face Tomorrow". This was much to the surprise and delight of the 300-strong congregation.

In one of my "funeral arrangement" conversations with John, I said that there would be one story I would not tell, as I was convinced everyone would have heard it – the one about Colin McGlashan. If the name is not familiar, the story may well be. Colin had suffered a head injury during a game and was lying concussed on the ground. The physiotherapist dutifully ran on to the pitch to attend to him. John shouted, "What's going on with him?" The concerned physiotherapist turned to John and said, "Gaffer, he doesn't know who he is!" He replied, "Well, tell him he's ****** Pele and get him back on!" This is perhaps the most well-known John Lambie story, which is why I suggested to him that I leave it out of the tribute. His response? "No you'll no! There'll be Whitburn people there who won't be football people – so you will tell it!" Of course, I did what I was told.

John also wanted Chic Charnley to say a few words at his funeral. I was concerned that Chic would break down in tears while trying to pay tribute to his beloved mentor, and a few times he nearly did, but he managed to get through it. I had many stories of my own to tell about John, which you will find in the chapter, "John Lambie - The Gaffer", but suffice to say it was one of the more light-hearted funerals I have conducted. Much as I was devastated at his passing, in line with John's instructions, there was much hilarity as I shared stories of John's personal and football life. He had certainly given me plenty of material to work with!

At the end of the service I showed some film clips of John in the dressing room after we had defeated St Mirren to clinch promotion to the Premier League in 2001 – obviously edited with a few bleeps. At the end of the footage, John finished his speech to the players by saying, "Right lads, that's me, I'm away…" And so that was what I closed his funeral service with. John always liked to have the final word. I trust the Gaffer would have approved of his funeral.

CHAPTER 18

HELPING FOOTBALLERS BEAT GAMBLING ADDICTION

One of the areas that I decided to upskill in is how to support footballers who want to recover from gambling addiction. Professional footballers are three times more likely to have gambling problems than other young men, according to research. A study conducted for the Professional Players' Federation shows 6.1% of sportsmen would be classed as problem gamblers compared with 1.9% in the general population of young men.

The study had a few more punches to deliver. One in ten said they gambled to "fit in", one in four said they were encouraged by teammates to do it, and nearly one in three thought their club's links with the gambling industry "encouraged" them to bet. It is also worth pointing out, that out of all the addiction categories, the highest suicide rate in the UK is among those addicted to gambling.

Over the years I have been asked to work with a number of players from different clubs who have had gambling addictions. I have been able to help most of them, but some have not been determined enough to take the steps necessary to manage, and ultimately overcome, this addiction. So why is gambling such a problem with footballers?

In my experience, the following is an A to E of why footballers are especially prone to gamble:

Adrenaline

Playing football gives you an incredible buzz. Adrenaline rushes through your veins as you get ready to leave the dressing room and walk out on to the pitch. As the game starts, you are desperate for a good first touch that settles you into the game. The adrenaline rush continues for 90 minutes and can last long after the game ends. It can take players many hours before they can relax, and for some, they may want the adrenaline rush to continue. Historically, some professional players indulged in cocaine and other drugs, but now, with random drug-testing, that is too risky. Gambling can be seen as the perfect substitute to cocaine.

Gambling gives an instant hit and the adrenaline rush is similar to that moment when you strike the ball, knowing it's on target and that's there's a good chance it's going to result in a goal if the goalkeeper cannot reach it.

One player I was supporting said to me that betting was like bidding for something on eBay. When you get to the final seconds of the bidding deadline, it's not actually about winning – it's the fact that you *might* win that produces adrenaline! Another player I worked with told me that when he was gambling, he felt like he was in a zone where nothing else existed except that gripping excitement that he might win. When he came out of that zone he realised the foolishness of what he had done. He was consumed with so much guilt and despair that he was determined not to gamble again – until the next time he was tempted.

Some gamblers go on binges. They can appear to be free from the addiction for months at a time, then perhaps there is a trigger that sets them off on a gambling spree. That trigger could be something that upsets them or it could even be a particular sporting event. Being able to recognise these triggers can be of great help because it enables them to see the temptation coming and to put things in place in order to deal with it. My advice when it comes to temptation of any kind is – don't fight it, flee from it.

Boredom

This is particularly the case for full-time professional players. I use the term "full-time" advisedly because I do not think being a footballer is actually a full-time occupation. If players are not involved in double training sessions then they should be encouraged to use their afternoons constructively – e.g. studying, learning a trade preparing for life outside football, coaching children, or visiting schools and hospitals. Many players lack a purpose outside of football and do not have anything else to focus on. They may have friends outside the game but it's likely that they will work a full day shift from 9am to 5pm so opportunities to socialise with others during the day may be limited. Some players simply have too much time on their hands. This can lead to boredom, which can lead to having unhealthy pastimes – including gambling.

Imagine the scenario: it's the night before a big match. Players are confined to their home or hotel. No alcohol. No junk food. To pass the time, footballers may watch television or play Xbox, but, for others, gambling could be seen as more exciting and interesting. Gambling addiction may be more prevalent among full-time players but many of the part-time players do not have a job outside of football. Therefore, they have time to fill and this can lead to gambling problems too.

Culture

A key reason why people gamble is because of the influence of their peers. I have helped a few players who started gambling through the influence of their fathers. However, for many, the main peer pressure has come from the gambling culture in the dressing room. Historically, this has been difficult to avoid. The majority of players used to gamble and pass on tips to each other. If you were a young impressionable player wanting to fit in and be accepted by your older teammates who you held in awe, it is understandable that you may have started to gamble with them – not realising that *you* had an addiction. It used to be a tradition, that when the manager announced the team, those not included in the squad would go off to the nearest bookmakers in order to "put their lines on".

Most managers do not want this culture in their dressing room any longer. Many even ban the "card schools" that were prevalent on bus journeys to away games. Players would sometimes appear to gamble for matchsticks. But, if one matchstick is actually worth £20 and you lose 10 matchsticks, it's hardly going to put you in a good frame of mind as you step off the team bus and prepare to play. Once you are in a card school it is very difficult to get out – particularly if you have won.

217

You need to give the others a chance to win their money back! I know of one player who was put under intolerable pressure from his teammates when he said he was leaving the card school after he had a decent windfall. I have also known of players who claimed they were alienated for not taking part in pre-match gambling activities.

I do think the gambling culture is beginning to wane a little bit, particularly in clubs with more foreign players, who often think gambling is a fool's game. Well, they do have a point – I have never once met a poor bookmaker but I have met many a broke footballer who has donated his significant earnings to the bookie.

This book is called "Confessions of a Football Chaplain" so here is an appropriate moment to share another one. When I was at Partick Thistle, a young player approached me before a game in which he was not taking part and said, "Rev, you've got contacts [pointing to the sky]. Here's my coupon. Tell me who the winners are going to be today." Now, I should point out that this was in the days before club employees were banned from betting on football matches. I really wanted to put this lad off gambling so I took three random fixtures and said, "Okay – Stenhousemuir home win, Dumbarton home win and East Fife away win." I assumed that this random selection would ensure he was not successful. I would then be able to tell him that not even I, with my contacts on high, could be a successful gambler, that it was a mug's game. You can guess what happened. Stenny won 3-0, Dumbarton won 4-0 and East Fife scored with the last kick of the game to win 3-2. He won £200 and tried to give me £20 as a thank you. I dutifully refused his reward and tried to advise him that this was a one-off bit of luck that would probably never happen again – but in truth I wasn't the best influence was I?

Determination

I think this is possibly the most significant reason why gambling addiction is prevalent among footballers. Footballers need to have a winning mentality in order to succeed. If a striker misses a scoring opportunity, he *has* to believe he will score next time. If the team loses a match, they *have* to believe they will win the next one. This is what keeps you going in the game – you need to have a positive, *winning* attitude! Now transfer this mentality into gambling and you can see why we have such a problem on our hands.

Gambling addicts are usually not focused on beating their addiction but on "beating the bookie". Often, all the gambler can think of is how that big win is going to undo all the damage his addiction has caused. Perhaps he has accrued so much gambling debt that he is never going to be able to recoup his losses through the legitimate means of earning money as a footballer. Just one win in the midst of many losses convinces him that he can win again. Indeed, probably the worst thing that ever happened to a gambling addict was that first win. Then there is also the competition in the dressing room. Players will boast of their gambling successes and that can encourage other teammates to try and better their winnings.

Now, combine that culture of gambling in a dressing room, with the determination to come out as top man in that environment, and it's a heady cocktail.

Ease of access

The temptation to gamble is all around players. Just look at the pitch-side advertisement boards and the TV adverts that are shown at half-time. They are continually bombarded with inducements from gambling companies. While they should not be betting on anything related to football, there are plenty of other options available to them. In the past, I took players round to gambling establishments to enable them to self-exclude themselves. They would be banned from betting in that particular bookmakers for a year and then have to repeat the process. However, because of the many opportunities to gamble online, and the many betting smart phone apps that are available, it is far more difficult to monitor someone's gambling activities.

How can I help?

In my experience, footballers who are gambling addicts have rarely approached me for help. However, parents, partners, managers and chief executives have asked me to provide support. The referral will often come when the player is under some kind of threat. He may be faced with being exposed to the media, or a potential relationship breakdown with his partner, or financial ruin, or he is getting threatened by loan sharks. In short, they have to hit rock bottom. Until that point, they may well think they are in control of the addiction, and probably be too proud or even too ashamed to seek help.

So what do I do when approached for help? Well, the first thing I do is explain that I am not the answer. I am not an expert. I cannot wave a magic wand and make the addiction disappear. I am not convinced there is anybody who can. The only person who can deal with the addiction is the player himself. It is not my responsibility to sort out the player's gambling problem. However, I can administer a form of first aid:

Signpost to other agencies

- CAP (Christians Against Poverty) is a Christian organisation that has a similar ethos to Sports Chaplaincy Scotland, in that they do not preach at people but give practical help, in this case, dealing with debt.

- Gamblers Anonymous has helped countless people, including footballers, manage the addiction. In my experience, however, some players feel that because of their fame they cannot be anonymous. They may also struggle to go along to meetings because of their training schedule.

- I also have contacts within the game, former players and managers who have overcame gambling addiction, who have offered personal support to players I work with.

CONFESSIONS OF A FOOTBALL CHAPLAIN

Insist on honesty – verified by affected people

Before I can begin to take a player forward, I need him to be completely honest about his situation – who he owes, how much he owes and who has been affected by his gambling debt – i.e. family, friends or teammates. This is a time when I need to show tough love and he needs to be desperate enough to place all his cards on the table. Excuse the terrible pun.

When he reveal the facts, I try to not look shocked and I am non-judgmental. I am very positive with him at this stage, because this shows tremendous humility, bravery and trust on his part to be willing to disclose this level of information – particularly if he is a high-profile player.

I also insist on ongoing honesty, including if he "has a blip and falls off the wagon", so to speak. If he does have a slip up and he tells me, I am never angry or disappointed with him. After all it's not my money he is wasting.

I see his honesty as a positive and vital step forward towards recovery. Bringing something into the light gives us an opportunity to see what it is we are fighting. It also provides the opportunity of receiving someone else's help in fighting it. If you try to fight anything in the dark, privately and alone, your chances of winning are very slim. Obviously, confidentiality is vital throughout the process of supporting a player, no one will ever find out who I have worked with unless the player makes it public.

Offer to negotiate with the creditors and form a repayment plan

Perhaps not everyone will feel comfortable with this but, because of my neutrality as a chaplain, I have no issues with contacting a player's creditors to negotiate the repayment of a debt. In my experience, most creditors are prepared to settle for a reasonable sum of money over a certain period, if it means they get their money back eventually. My aim is always to make sure creditors are paid back in full. However, if the situation has spiralled out of control, and has become unmanageable, I would possibly signpost the player to an organisation such as CAP.

Form a budgeting plan

In previous roles in my life, I have helped many people learn how to form a budget. I remember one young single mum who approached me for help. She was in debt and she could not see a way out of it. She had a young pre-school son whom she wanted to provide for, so she worked as a child-minder, in a bid to earn money. When I looked at her income and outgoings I told her that, within a year, I would not only have her debt free but she was going to take her little boy on holiday abroad. She actually laughed in disbelief, but a year later, she and her son were laughing on a beach in Spain. Since that time, she has helped other friends learn the joy of budgeting. Some players have never learned to take responsibility for their finances. I seek to help them realise that the money they earn needs to have a purpose and is not simply "disposable income". We discuss that later under "The A and E of addressing the problem."

Restrict access to money

This can be a big challenge. I try to make sure all potential betting opportunities are closed down. This will entail the removal of access to all his and that of his friends and families' bank accounts, credit cards etc.

It may be reasonable to appoint a Power of Attorney who establishes and administers the repayment plan and budgeting plan. That person will allocate to the player what he needs to live on – though everything he spends needs to be evidenced by the production of a receipt. This responsible person needs to show tough love and not be easily manipulated. It could be the player's parent, partner, club secretary or friend – never me though!

It may also be appropriate for the player to stand up in front of the rest of the lads in the dressing room and disclose his addiction, so that they know not to lend him money or give him "tips." On a players' night out, another teammate might hold the recovering gambling addict's spending money.

What is very important is that the player himself identifies every possible source of money he can obtain, and makes sure that source is stopped. He does this by telling potential lenders that on no account should they give him money for anything, regardless of what he claims he needs it for.

Establish Accountability

The player needs someone to whom he can safely confess failings. This could be the club chaplain. The player needs to be continually reassured that the enemy is the gambling addiction, not him, and that you are fighting this enemy together. It is also helpful to remind the player that if he slips up, it's no skin off your nose – it's not your money he is losing!

One player I was helping, phoned me up one morning to confess that during the night he had stolen his partner's bank card, went online and gambled away £500. He was in a dreadful state, consumed with guilt and self-hatred. However, I encouraged him that we had actually made some great progress. He had been honest enough to tell his partner and me what he had done. Now, the next stage of his recovery was for him to tell us when he was being tempted to gamble.

This particular player started to keep a journal in which he charted out his life, noting the times, feelings or situations when he was prone to gambling. This helped him identify triggers of which he was not previously conscious.

In this last section we will look at the **A to E of Addressing the Problem.**

Adrenaline – Find an alternative buzz

What could the player be focussing on that would take his mind off gambling, but still gives him an adrenaline rush? What makes him come alive and leads to fulfilment outside of football and gambling?

Footballers are often obsessive – this can actually help them become dedicated in their pursuit of success. What positive activity could they start to obsess about? One player I worked with said that he could not think of anything outside of football and gambling that interested him. I asked him to use the following week to try and notice something in which he might take up an interest. When we met up, he told me that he had watched a cookery programme, and thought, "I could do that!" From that point, he became obsessed about cooking healthy food. Another player I worked with showed tremendous acumen for numbers and so I encouraged him to take a course in accountancy. I suppose you might think it would be difficult to get an adrenaline rush from being an accountant, but you never know!

Boredom – Find a purpose outside of football

It is really important to help the player fill his spare time with meaningful, positive and productive activity. Having a well-planned and structured day every day is essential. As mentioned before, full-time footballers can have a lot of time on their hands and so they are limited in what they can do recreationally. For example, they cannot go ice skating, rock climbing or participate in any other sport where they may incur an injury. Some players will perhaps go for a round of golf, a game of snooker or play FIFA on the Xbox, but their choices are fairly limited.

The irony of this situation is that, when their career is over, they could face even more boredom, because they are not prepared for life after playing football. PFA Scotland does its best to encourage and facilitate players to take college courses or learn trades so that they are not dependant on the game for a living in the long-term. After all, only so many can go on to coaching and management. Gambling requires intelligence. How can we can encourage the player to channel his intelligence elsewhere? Is there something they could be doing that builds their confidence and dispels the myth that they may have believed about themselves that they are "a bit thick"? I believe that everyone is a genius. All of us are brilliant at something. We encourage our chaplains to help players identify their God-created genius outside of football.

Culture – Friendship re-evaluation

The player may need to reconsider his friendship groups if his contemporaries are leading him astray. One player I helped was desperate to kick his habit, but he admitted he had a friend who was also a gambling addict. When he spent time with him, he invariably ended up going along to the bookmaker's with him. Again, some tough love was required. I advised the player to give his friend an ultimatum. Either he acknowledged his addiction and sought help too, or they went their separate ways. His friend was on the phone to me shortly afterwards, acknowledging his addiction and asking for help. I would love all stories to end like this, but the reality is that most addicts will need to cut off some friends. I would encourage them to socialise with people who do not gamble, or even better, get alongside other players who have conquered the gambling habit.

Determination – Focus on other goals

I encourage players to set goals beyond playing football, particularly financial goals – buying a house or saving for a special holiday. One player I worked with had agreed to allow his mother to control his finances, and he received a small amount of pocket money from her. Each time I saw him, he would tell me with great glee that he was continuing to save his money as he was aiming to buy a place of his own. He is the type of lad who will probably buy a place for his mother too. This is something worth mentioning: I cannot think of one gambling addict I have helped who I would not describe as kind-hearted and good-natured. The addiction may have driven them to do terrible things, but in the cold light of day they are usually really decent guys. Like I said, it is the addiction I hate, not them. I try to encourage the player to become excited about new goals for their lives.

Forming a repayment/budgeting plan with them can really help because, as they repay their debt, this releases more money that they can save. As they see their cash building up and working for them, they become really encouraged.

Ease of Access – Form good habits

What else can they do that is easy for them to access, and that can become a good alternative habit? I want to take them to a place where they are automatically changing their lifestyle without even realising they are even doing it. I sometimes use an illustration. Let's say you get a new pair of slippers for Christmas. You like them but so does your pet dog, and he decides that they are the best thing he has been able to chew for a while. If you try and take the slippers from him, he will perhaps think it's a game, and he may be reluctant to let go. However, if you put one of his dog treats beside the slipper, the likelihood is that the dog will focus on the snack and abandon the slipper, so you can simply take it away without a fight. What I am trying to do is help the player find something with which he can replace the addiction, without having to make a conscious effort.

I also encourage them to use a technique called "the motivational pinch point." When they recognise the trigger to gamble, they physically pinch themselves, which triggers a pre-programmed automatic response to that temptation e.g. phone someone, go for a walk, play some uplifting music. Anything that is a positive, productive distraction may work.

The bottom line is that anyone can overcome a gambling addiction if they really want to, if they are genuinely prepared to pay the price, and do what it takes. Chaplains are prepared to walk with them through that process.

CHAPTER 19

POSITIVE MENTAL HEALTH SCOTLAND

During one season, when I was chaplain at Partick Thistle, the stadium announcer temporarily stepped down from his role. I was asked to take his place until they found a replacement. I am familiar with public speaking so I relished the prospect of doing this – and I thoroughly enjoyed it. I was free to announce in my own style, but there was one tradition I was asked to retain. When our midfielder Martin Hardie scored, I was expected to loudly announce, "And the scorer for the Jags – Big! Mad! Mental! Martin Hardeeeeee!" Scottish football has never been renowned for political correctness. Martin was not offended by this announcement. Quite the contrary – he basked in his reputation of being perceived as a "hard man". I remember a centre half at Thistle whose nickname was "Psycho" and this was not meant as an insult either. Indeed, the player accepted this moniker as a compliment. It was a recognition of his tough and fearless style of play.

It should not, therefore, come as a surprise, that mental health has not always been fully understood and recognised in football circles. This is reflected by the following scenario that took place a number of years ago. I was asked by a manager to give some pastoral support to one of his players. Here is how the conversation went:

"Aye Mark, it's the wee man – he's got mental health…"

"Oh really? You do realise that you have mental health too?"

"What? No I don't, I'm absolutely fine!"

"Oh you do, and what's more, so do I!"

"Seriously? You'd never think it wee man, you seem okay to me. How do you cope?"

"I actually cope very well. Mate, mental health is our psychological wellbeing and we've all got it. It affects how we're thinking, feeling and behaving. But it's not the same thing as mental illness."

"Aye, alright. Anyway, will you get inside his head and sort him for me?"

Pragmatic and straight to the point – that's football managers for you.

Your mental health affects how you cope with everyday life and everything it throws at you. Imagine that your eyes are your window on the world. Your mental wellbeing is like a set of venetian blinds. If your mental health is good, the blinds are open and up. You are able to see upward and forward – you have hope and optimism. You are able to see clearly outside – you have perspective. There is plenty of light in the room. However, if your mental health is in poor condition, the blinds are down and half shut. It's difficult to have hope and see a way forward. It's hard to see things objectively. And the room seems dark. Words that are spoken to you, which are normally water off a duck's back, now get right under your skin. Circumstances that you would normally be able to cope with, now appear overwhelming.

In 2014, I was involved in a serious mental health crisis intervention with a player. This experience was to have a profound impact on me. It would also lead to positive new developments within Scottish football.

I would normally retain the anonymity of those involved in the following story, in order to maintain confidentiality. However, the respective people have given me permission to mention them by name. One Thursday afternoon, I received a phone call from my good friend Grant Murray, who at that time, was manager of Raith Rovers. He was deeply distressed because one of his players had attempted to complete suicide that morning by trying to drown himself in the River Forth. The police and paramedics had left the player's home after they were satisfied that he had physically recovered. However, when he phoned his manager, it was clear that he remained in a poor mental condition. Grant asked if I would go and visit him. I cannot tell you how nervous I was about this. What if I said the wrong thing? However, I obliged and went to see the player. Thankfully, I had a good understanding of the issues that had led to the marked downturn in the player's mental health, and so I was able to provide some appropriate help there and then. He subsequently saw a doctor, was diagnosed with depression and was provided with further support. The next morning, Grant phoned me up and asked how the visit to the player went. I told him that I felt the intervention had been successful, but that the lad would need further help. Grant's next question might make him appear to be ruthless and uncaring, but I can assure you this was not the case. It was actually out of deep concern for the player's wellbeing that he asked me, "Should I play him tomorrow?

I really need him but I don't want to push him over the edge or put too much pressure on him." It was a very good question and one that I have been asked several times since. My answer was, "If you think he is physically fit and match-sharp – play him! Given that he has been vulnerable, honest and open with you about his weaknesses, if you still pick him, I think he'll run through a brick wall for you." I was more than a little nervous about offering this advice. What if the player had a nightmare of a game? It would be my fault. However, Grant took my advice and the player, Christian Nade, scored a vital equaliser in a 1-1 draw with Hibernian. As a former Hearts player, it would be fair to assume that he really enjoyed that goal! Christian and I became good friends and we remain in contact today. He has been very honest with the media about his battle with mental illness and this has encouraged other players to be open about their struggles too. While I was able to provide initial and ongoing support to Christian, it was important that he went to see a doctor. Since then, we have talked at length about the practical life adjustments he needs to make in order to remain in good mental health.

As a result of this intervention, I felt that I needed to be upskilled in the area of mental health. So, I attended the two day NHS Scotland mental health first aid course. The instructor was Anne Mathie. She was a fount of knowledge and delivered the training with such passion. The course informs delegates on the following issues: what mental health actually is; attitudes towards mental health issues; how to support someone recovering from a mental illness; the impact of various addictions on mental health; basic suicide intervention; listening skills; understanding depression, anxiety and psychosis – and how to offer first aid to someone experiencing the effects of these illnesses. Essentially, people are trained to spot the physical, emotional, behavioural and verbal signs that all is not mentally well with someone. It provides the delegates with the knowledge, skills and confidence to approach someone if they are concerned about their mental wellbeing and it equips them to be a bridge to appropriate help. Although I should say that the training does not equip anyone to be a mental health expert, a counsellor or a therapist. A mental health first aider should never approach someone and tell them they have a mental problem – it is made very clear that only a doctor can diagnose such an illness.

Anne also happened to be one of NHS Scotland's national trainers of mental health first aid instructors. At the end of the two day course, she shocked me by suggesting that I should consider becoming an instructor and then apply the course to a football context. At the time I was very unsure, as this was well out of my comfort zone. I had never worked in the field of mental health before. However, Anne reminded me that I had been providing pastoral support for nearly 20 years within Scottish football at that time, so I was well-placed to understand the unique pressures that can have a negative impact on the mental health of those working within the game. So, I applied to NHS Scotland to be trained. I was accepted, and I subsequently qualified as an instructor in the autumn of 2015.

CONFESSIONS OF A FOOTBALL CHAPLAIN

I will be eternally grateful to Anne, because she took me under her wing and mentored me for two years. I felt so nervous and inadequate when I started to deliver the course, but Anne was a constant source of encouragement and inspiration. Through her, my knowledge and confidence grew to the point that I was able to operate as a solo instructor and also support a number of people in Scottish football who have struggled with their mental health.

Through Anne's encouragement, I set up my own mental health training business, Positive Mental Health Scotland, through which I deliver the mental health first aid course and other shorter workshops. A key person in the development of my business has been my good friend Steven Turnbull. When Danny Lennon was manager of St Mirren, I introduced him to Steven who, alongside other roles, is a mental health coach and a sports psychologist. Steven went on to work with Danny and the team, playing an important role in the lead up to the club's Scottish League Cup triumph against Hearts in 2013 – the first time in Saints' history that they had won this cup. As well as helping me to set up my business, Steven also trained my wife, Aileen, to be a mental health coach, and since then she has helped many people, including those involved in football, enjoy improved mental wellbeing. Now, as a partner in the business, Aileen is helping me develop the services we can offer.

I deliver the mental health first aid course through the Scottish Professional Football League Trust and the Chris Mitchell Foundation, two organisations that I have great respect for.

The SPFL Trust is an independent, registered charity that works in partnership with all 42 SPFL clubs to develop community activities across Scotland. Using the power of football, they have empowered and enabled professional Scottish football clubs to positively impact their local communities.

It is reckoned that they have reached out to 84% of the Scottish population. For example, the FFIT programme (Football Fans In Training) has been one of the most successful ventures in tackling obesity in Scotland. I have heard countless testimonies from people who have lost significant weight and, more importantly, gained enormous confidence as a result of this programme.

I have a close working relationship with SPFL Trust CEO, Nicky Reid, and we saw a great need for clubs to have people trained in mental health first aid. To us, it seemed incongruous that every football team in Scotland was expected to have a first aider to provide initial help for someone with a physical injury, yet there was not the same provision of a mental health first aider.

For me, I wanted to take it a step further. Rather than having a single mental health first aider at every club in Scotland, I wanted to see the entire culture changed. I long to see the stigma of mental illness in Scottish football obliterated, and for that to happen we needed to train as many people as possible within clubs. This was going to be a big ask, especially financially.

This is where the Chris Mitchell Foundation came in. The charity was founded in memory of Chris Mitchell, a well-known Scottish professional footballer, who tragically died by suicide in 2016. Chris was a hard-working and talented full back/midfielder. He was solid in defence and a great crosser of the ball. He played for Scotland in schoolboy internationals and also at under-21 level, winning seven caps. Eddie May brought Chris to the Falkirk Youth Academy in 2006, and it was there he developed into an excellent player.

He played 50 times for Falkirk. In 2011, Chris moved to Bradford City, at that time, of the English Second Division. He and his Falkirk teammate Mark Stewart, who I knew well from his time at Partick Thistle, signed for the club at the same time. After one season, Allan Johnston, the manager of Queen of the South, brought him back to Scotland. And what a great signing Chris turned out to be. He was very popular with the supporters, receiving several Player of the Year awards, and he was also selected by PFA Scotland for the Division Team of the Year.

Chris spent three seasons with the Doonhamers and enjoyed considerable success. He helped Queens win the Scottish Second Division. They also won the lower leagues' "double" by winning the Challenge Cup. I was at that game, supporting their opponents, Partick Thistle. After extra time the game was still tied at 1-1, but the Doonhamers won the match on penalties 6-5, Chris scoring the penultimate one.

At the time I was absolutely devastated. Now that I know how much that victory meant to Chris and his family, it certainly takes the pain of defeat away from me.

Queen of the South continued their upward trajectory the following season, aided in great measure by the solid performances of Chris. They finished fourth in the Scottish First Division, now the Championship, only denied a place in the top tier by a play-off defeat. Sadly, this was to be the final season at Queens for Chris, due to back injury problems requiring surgery. As a result, appearances were restricted.

Having played 85 times for the Dumfries side, at the start of season 2015-16, Chris signed for Clyde as a part-timer. At this stage in his career he was now having to think about employment outside football. He secured a good job working with his uncle, so, with his back causing increasing problems, he retired at the end of that January. He had played 16 times for Clyde. However, he found the transition to life outside football extremely difficult and he developed depression. His girlfriend and family tried their utmost to provide the best support they could for Chris, but tragically he completed suicide on 7 May 2016, aged 27.

I did not know Chris but I was introduced to his family by our Ross County chaplain, Iain MacAskill, who lives near them. I formed a very close bond with these incredible people. Out of their own unspeakable grief, they birthed the Chris Mitchell Foundation in his memory. One of the purposes of the charity is to enable people working in Scottish football to be trained up in mental health first aid.

It has been one of the greatest honours and privileges of my life to work with Chris's family to achieve their objectives.

Through the SPFL Trust and Chris Mitchell Foundation I have delivered mental health first aid training to over 500 people who work in Scottish football, including representatives from every one of the 42 SPFL clubs. The delegates have included directors, managers, coaches, players, doctors, sport psychologists, physiotherapists, kit men, groundsmen, wellbeing officers, and, as you may have expected – chaplains. Part of the chaplain's role is to provide pastoral support for the mental, emotional and spiritual wellbeing of everyone connected with a football club. Therefore, the mental health first aid course is part of their preparation for appointment.

Most of those courses have been delivered in the SPFL boardroom at Hampden Park in Glasgow. It's perhaps not surprising then, that the Glasgow-based professional clubs have had the biggest representation. To date, Celtic have sent 18 staff members on the course – more than any other club. Rangers and Partick Thistle are not far behind, having both sent 16 delegates. In order to encourage people from other parts of the country to complete the course, the following clubs have hosted the training days at their stadiums – Aberdeen, Hearts, Hibernian, St Johnstone, Inverurie Locos and Spartans.

Why have so many Scottish football clubs sent people to be trained in mental health first aid? Why not simply have one mental health first aid officer in each club? Well, I could imagine a player going to see the doctor or physiotherapist if he had a physical problem, but I am not so sure that he would approach a mental health care provider. There are two reasons for this.

Firstly, if a player is physically injured, he can point to the area of his body where he is experiencing pain or discomfort. He can usually define and articulate what is wrong with him. However, if someone is experiencing the onset of a mental illness, especially for the first time, it is unlikely that they will know what is wrong with them. They will suspect something is not right, but they may not be able to explain what is going on. So they may suffer in silence. However, if many people at a club are trained as mental health first aiders, there is more of a chance that someone will pick up on the early signs of poor mental health and that this will lead to an appropriate intervention, pointing the player in the right direction for help.

The second reason why a player is unlikely to approach a mental health care provider is because of the stigma of mental illness. If you are a footballer, you accept that there is a risk of physical injury. It is usually obvious how an injury has happened and the effects of the injury are ordinarily clear to be seen. However, a mental illness may not have an obvious cause and the effects of it may be unseen, so there is every possibility that someone will simply feel weak or stupid. They may castigate themselves for not feeling at their best "for no good reason". Personally, I do not see mental illness any differently to physical injury. If many people in a football club are trained in mental health first aid, it can help change the culture of the club and remove the stigma.

Hibernian asked me to deliver the two day course to a group of key staff at their training centre. The club has developed an excellent mental wellbeing strategy, which seeks to eradicate the stigma of mental illness and provide support around the mental health of their players and staff. I believe they have developed a model that other clubs could follow.

Here is a question worth considering. If a player did realise that he was experiencing a mental illness, who would he talk to about it? I would suggest that, in most cases, he would be reticent to talk to his manager. Perhaps he would be concerned that his manager would drop him from the team, perceiving him to be a weak link. What about telling one of his teammates? Again, I would suggest this is unlikely. He may be concerned that his teammate would consider him pathetic, or that the rest of the dressing room might find out and he could become the butt of their jokes. Worse still, what if that teammate becomes his opponent the following season? The former colleague may whisper insults in his ear, hoping to get an angry reaction, which could lead to a red card.

To illustrate this, David Cox is a Scottish professional footballer who has been very honest in the media about his struggles with mental illness. This has not always engendered the sympathy and support his openness deserves. David has been goaded by opponents and verbally abused by supporters. He has shown great bravery and resilience but he should not have to put up with that kind of behaviour. David has had good relationships with a number of chaplains at clubs he has played for and on a number of occasions they have been a lifeline to him in terms of his mental wellbeing.

CONFESSIONS OF A FOOTBALL CHAPLAIN

The chaplain is ideally placed to provide that kind of support, because, as I have already noted, their role is not performance-based. They will listen to everything confidentially, with the caveat that if the player indicates that they are going to seriously harm themselves or someone else, the chaplain will need to inform the appropriate person. Given that the chaplain may well be a player's first port of call in a mental health crisis, it is essential for them to complete the mental health first aid course so that they know how to handle such a situation and what appropriate signposting measures they should take.

One of the challenges I have found in delivering the mental health first aid course is that it lasts for two days and some clubs have felt unable to release certain staff for that length of time. As a result, I have developed a one day course specifically for football clubs and youth academies that is CPD approved. This has led to opportunities to deliver in-house training for clubs such as Celtic, Hearts, Aberdeen and also the Scottish FA. Further afield, I have had the privilege of providing mental health awareness training for Liverpool and the English FA. Subsequent engagements with other organisations in England, Wales and France have caused me to consider changing the name of my business to Positive Mental Health International! I am also conscious that there are many part-time and amateur clubs whose personnel are only available in the evening, so I have developed a three hour training session in mental health awareness. I want as many people as possible to have a good working knowledge around the subject.

CONFESSIONS OF A FOOTBALL CHAPLAIN

As I have developed my work in the field of mental health, my role as Scottish Director of Sports Chaplaincy UK has become part-time. I view my two roles as parallel railroad tracks – there is great synergy between both lines of work because they involve being concerned for the psychological wellbeing of sports people rather than merely the performances or results they produce.

There is another reason why I am passionate about mental wellbeing. I did not mention this when writing about the mental health first aid course I attended in 2015, but I found the experience to be personally cathartic. You see, until then, I had been too embarrassed to admit to anyone that four years previously, in 2011, I had suffered with depression. At the course I attended, I was publically honest about my experience for the first time, as I openly shared with the rest of the delegates. At the time of my illness, I had no idea that was what was wrong with me. I started to notice that I was not my normal self when I lost my appetite – I lost a stone in weight in six months. I was finding it very difficult to fall asleep and I woke up throughout the night, having repetitive thoughts – it was like driving round a roundabout but not being able to find an exit. My energy levels were unusually very low. At times, I was demotivated and I had no enthusiasm for that which I normally enjoyed. What really worried me was that I was finding it very difficult to process basic information. At times, when people were speaking to me, it wasn't that their words were "in one ear and out of the other", it seemed more like their words were swirling around outside of my head and I could not process them in my brain.

I actually wondered at one point if I had suffered a mini-stroke because I found it very hard to function mentally at times. When I was alone, sometimes I burst into tears for no apparent reason. When I was in the company of others, I put in a huge amount of effort to appear happy and energetic, because I did not want anyone to suspect that there was something wrong with me. But I was usually utterly exhausted after putting up a façade. In fact, I would be so tired, I did not have the energy to answer my phone or reply to emails. Everything became a huge effort – even life itself.

I did not want to go to the local doctor, and not because I did not trust her. It was more because I was anxious about being spotted going into our local medical practice. I was convinced that everybody would talk about me and say, "He's not right in the head. What help could he possibly be to anyone else? Who would go to him with their problems when he is screwed up?" So I suffered in silence. I did not want my wife to know there was something wrong, because I did not want to worry her and I could not explain the problem anyway. When she expressed any concerns to me about my mood swings I would become very self-defensive and irritable.

I began to feel that I was a liability and the world would be better off without me. I did not think about suicide *per se*, but I longed for death. I wanted to go to sleep and not wake up. A friend of mine intervened, but I don't know if he realised that this was what he was doing. I was sitting in the passenger seat of his car as we were driving to a football match at Firhill. He turned to me and said, "Mark, I hope you don't mind me saying this, but I've noticed you've not been yourself for a while. When you smile, your mouth is smiling but your eyes aren't. And when you're in company, it's like you're on a different planet, you seem really disconnected. I'm really concerned about you – is everything okay?"

I had been rumbled. I tried to tell him, as honestly as I could, what I was experiencing. The conclusion was obvious – I needed help. However, I still did not want to go to my local medical practice. Thankfully, I had a friend who was a doctor, to whom I spoke "off the record". I was shocked with the diagnosis – depression. Me? Depressed? Surely that only happened to pessimistic and melancholic people? I was the opposite. I was optimistic and sanguine – it helps when you follow Partick Thistle. However, I had to accept that I was depressed and probably had been so for some time. I confess that I was terrified of taking anti-depressants because this would mean that the conversation with my doctor-friend could no longer be "off the record". A diagnosis of depression would now be "on my record." It was not only the stigma of having a mental illness that caused me to be reticent about medication – I knew people who had experienced negative side-effects as a result of taking certain pills. Now that I understand how anti-depressants work, I would have no hesitation in recommending that you take them if your doctor thinks they are necessary, though I would also advise you to do your own research into the medication you have been prescribed.

I discovered that there were also other potential means of tackling the illness, like cognitive behavioural therapy. CBT is based on the concept that your thoughts, feelings, physical sensations and actions are interconnected. Negative thoughts and feelings can trap you in a vicious cycle. CBT shows you how to challenge and change negative thought-patterns to improve the way you feel. I chose to try self-help CBT and it really helped me overcome depression. I also became more self-aware. In the past, bouts of depression felt like an overwhelming "tsunami wave", debilitating me to the point that I found it very difficult to function mentally and even physically. However, I learned to spot these "waves" at a distance, and I learned different skills that effectively erected "flood barriers".

I also became more intentional and proactive in looking after my mental wellbeing. Would you not agree that it's better to build a fence at the top of a hill than to have to go to a hospital at the bottom? People seem to invest increasing amounts of time, money and energy in order to protect and improve their physical health. Is it not about time we did the same for our mental health? We could be talking more about mental illness prevention rather than simply mental illness intervention.

Delegates who have attended the mental health first aid course often ask, "What's next? Is there a follow up course?" At present I am developing one. Since completing my Masters degree in 2016, I have been examining studies on the brain chemicals dopamine, serotonin, oxytocin and endorphins. My research has involved looking at how exercise, a healthy balanced diet, good sleep hygiene, periods of rest, uplifting music, laughter, positive relationships, doing what you are good at/enjoy and expressing thankfulness can facilitate the increase and release of these neurotransmitters and help us enjoy *positive* mental health. Just as I investigated the potential benefits of taking supplements to help build up my physical immunity system, I have also done so with regard to the building up of my mental immunity system. I will not go into details now, but I have personally benefited from taking Vitamins B12 and D3 and also Omega 3 supplements. Maybe that is for another book...

I would like to close this chapter by inviting a former Scotland international player to tell her story. My wife and I have absolutely loved working with Becca Dempster when she was a player but also in the aftermath of her career. I hope that her account will encourage anyone involved in football who has struggled with their mental health. There is hope.

Since the age of 4 years old, I knew I wanted to be a football player and I dedicated the next 25 years of my life to achieving everything I could within the sport at the time. However, my journey was not an easy one. At age 19, I had already represented Scotland at under-15, under-17 and was excelling at under-19 level, becoming the top goal scorer in the European Championships and named in the top European players to watch in the future. I was now breaking into the senior Scotland squad. However, in the background, in the midst of all my achievements, I was really battling the negative thoughts in my head. I was diagnosed with depression and I was blind to all the positive things happening for me.

I became very unhappy within myself and began hurting myself. I felt there was no light at the end of the tunnel. Meanwhile I was breaking into the Senior Scotland National team and acquired four caps. I seemed to think that if I became someone on the football stage, everything in my head would be sorted. However, the pressure I put on myself became unbearable and I made the decision to leave the Scottish Sports Institute and international setup. For the next few years, I had the belief in my head that this was just who I was and life was going to be miserable no matter how much love my parents showed me.

After a really tough break up with the person I thought I was going to spend my life with, I was offered the chance to go to Italy to play professionally. Italy was such an incredible life experience. I played alongside and against true legends of the Italian game and met so many amazing people, who thoroughly immersed me in the Italian lifestyle, which was my first real cultural experience out with Scotland.

As much as there were moments I was enjoying these new experiences, for the most part, I was just going through the motions on and off the pitch. I felt lost and detached from my physical being. I just couldn't understand why I wasn't filled with happiness and pride. I was 25 years old and had already achieved everything I ever wanted to within my football career. I remember sitting on the bathroom floor of the house I shared with some of my Italian teammates, my arms messed up from the lighter next to me, thinking there was just no point in carrying on.

I managed to stick out the season with the help and support of the club and my teammates then headed home to recoup with my parents. I was offered a professional contract in Australia soon after returning home and felt after the security of being with my parents for a few months, I had the bravery and strength to give it a go. My first six months were very similar to Italy. There were many great experiences but again, inside I was miserable. I often put myself in dangerous situations and inevitably, my parents paid to fly me home.

I was broken and did not know who to turn to for help. I had already forked out hundreds of pounds on therapy, psychologists, psychiatrists and counsellors over the years. Although I was no longer involved with the national set up, I decided to get in contact with my coach from under-19 level, Shelley Kerr, now, of course, the Senior National Team manager. Shelley had supported me throughout and although 1 was struggling off the pitch, she always managed to get the best out of me on it. I am so glad I contacted her as she called me almost immediately, despite her busy schedule, and put me in contact with Mark, who was the chaplain for the national team at the time.

Although I was in Aberdeen, Mark drove from Glasgow to meet with me the very next day! We sat in a sea front café and 1 opened up to this wee bald Glaswegian stranger about how I had been feeling. Little did I know that he would become such an iconic feature of my life. To my amazement, Mark opened up to me about his own personal mental health struggles.

This instantly gave me hope, because he was so smiley, happy and enthusiastic. I longed to feel that way. He assured me that it takes commitment and hard work to fight through these challenges, but it is absolutely doable. Since that day, Mark has remained in my life and I genuinely can't get rid of the guy! He sees so much potential in me and fills me with desire to fight back.

Not long after, I headed for another contract in Brisbane, Australia. This time I went over with a new outlook. I didn't focus solely on the football side of things. Mark had taught me that the sport doesn't define who I am and that I should find happiness in the little things. This is exactly what I did for the next six months. Every day, I made a point of heading for the water's edge to read, write and listen to positive stories, thoughts and hopes for the future. These six months were the happiest I had felt since childhood. I had avoided putting pressure on myself on the football pitch and just started to enjoy the game I had fell in love with as a child. It was so refreshing and I truly believe I wouldn't have allowed my Brisbane experience to be all that it was without Marks input.

Unfortunately, when I returned to Scotland, I fell back into my old ways. I was putting pressure on myself to be 'Becca the Footballer' again. I felt I should be in my prime but recurring injuries meant my body couldn't keep up with my football brain. It became very frustrating for me when I saw what I wanted to do (e.g. the through ball I wanted to play or getting on the end of a cross) but my body wouldn't allow it to happen.

CONFESSIONS OF A FOOTBALL CHAPLAIN

Football had lost its spark for me, which I was struggling to come to terms with. All my life, I had been 'Becca the Footballer', but now I was just Becca and I didn't know how to be just Becca. Although my decision to completely walk away from playing football had slowly been approaching in my head, it was very sudden. I felt I still had a few good seasons left in me at a high level, so it was a tough decision to ultimately make in the end. On one hand it felt unnatural and strange not to have training to attend, but on the other hand I oddly felt relieved I no longer had that commitment. It was almost a sense of freedom. But I did not know what to do with my freedom.

I had dedicated 25 years of my life to football, I didn't know how to live without it. A big part of me still doesn't as all this happened only a year or so previous to this book being written. Mark and his wife are still working very closely with me to help me understand my worth in the world without football defining me. I have made massive progress since Mark came in to my life.

Along with the support of him and my parents, I am on a good path. I still have a huge amount of work to do. However, the realization that I don't have to feel this way and I can be happy as Becca is so rewarding and I am so ready and willing to put in the hard work to keep improving as a person and achieving other things in life.

CHAPTER 20

FROM FAIRLIE TO FIRHILL VIA FAITH

At this juncture, I would like to give you some of my back story – it may well shock you! You might have assumed that, because I am a chaplain, I have a Christian background. Far from it. I have already established that my footballing ability was very limited, but at the age of 16, I would have said that there was more likelihood of me being called in to the Scotland squad than there was of me joining the "God squad".

At that time in my life I was an atheist. In fact, when I was in fifth year at Largs Academy, my English teacher christened me the "Antichrist" because I was so antagonistic towards religious people, and Christians in particular. This was due to my upbringing. My dad did not want me to connect with the church in any way. I was not even allowed to join the Boys Brigade because he perceived it to be a religious organisation.

So, at the age of 14, I did what most teenagers do – I rebelled. In my case, I attended a local church. However, after a year of suffering hard pews and boring sermons, I decided Christianity was not for me. This was when I became particularly antagonistic, engaging in verbal jousts with members of the aforementioned "God Squad" at school. This appears to be what gained me the reputation of being an "Antichrist."

I did wonder if there was any other religion worth looking into. However, after reading other books on various faiths, I came to the conclusion that religion was for weak-minded people who could not think for themselves. In my opinion, religious people were brainwashed, controlled, suppressed and exploited. They were not prepared to take responsibility for their lives so they trusted in an imaginary higher power to do for them what they were too lazy to do for themselves. It was a form of escapism. Further to that, in my view, religion caused nothing but trouble.

As a teenager, I followed the same pursuits as my friends – namely girls and alcohol. I was not particularly successful at the former, and the latter led me into a lot of trouble, including getting grounded by my parents for three months. If that sounds rather draconian – I had traded in my tennis racket for a half-bottle of vodka. Oh yes, and I became so drunk that I lay down on the main road, so that a neighbour nearly ran over me with her car.

During fifth year at school, a friend of mine shocked and horrified me by telling me he had "become a Christian". At first I thought it was just a phase he was going through. Like me, he had been a punk and then a mod, so now that he had turned to religion, I was confident it would not last. I was wrong.

31 May 1980 will be forever etched on my memory. It was a beautiful sunny day and I was relaxing in my back garden listening to music by Bob Marley and the Wailers, eagerly anticipating seeing them live in concert at the old Glasgow Apollo Theatre six weeks later. That gig, on 10 July 1980, remains the best concert I have ever attended and roots reggae remains my favourite musical genre to this day.

I had left school that week – what a wonderful feeling. After the summer, I was due to begin studies at Caledonian University, Glasgow in Computing. I was happy and optimistic about my future. I certainly did not feel there was anything missing in my life or that I had any needs of a spiritual nature,

My Christian friend knew that any attempt to bring me to a church service would be in vain, so that day, he tried another tack – he invited me along to his church youth club, the carrot being that they had decent table tennis facilities. You know how much I enjoy a game of table tennis, so I decided to go – but I intended to make him sorry he invited me. I was going to hammer these "Bible bashers" at table tennis. I also intended to ask really awkward questions of everyone who spoke to me. Basically, I would do what was necessary so they would never invite me back. There was no way they were going to convert me, that was for sure.

I won all my table tennis matches. I defeated the Christians in most of the debates I started with them. However, there were certain things I could not contest. How do you argue with someone who tells you they have had a life-transforming encounter with God? I knew everyone there and I had to admit, I had observed genuinely positive changes in their lives. They were convinced they were connected to God, and confident that they would eventually be going to heaven. Why did I not have this assurance when I had tried Christianity before? They gave me a simple answer – I had not actually been a Christian. I had attempted to be *religious* but these people talked of having a *relationship* with God.

In truth, even though I had attended a church it had not really made any difference to me. As someone said to me, "Going to McDonald's doesn't make you a Big Mac!"

I was so interested in listening to their experiences that I missed my last bus home. The leader of the group, Maurice Craig, was also my Physics teacher at school. He drove me back to my house and gave me some leaflets that explained how I could get to know Jesus. When I told my parents where I had been and that I was considering becoming a Christian, it's fair to say they were not too impressed. I think my dad would have responded better had I told him I was a drug addict! He took the leaflets, tore them up and threw them in the bin. He warned me off getting involved with "that lot". He believed he was acting in what he considered to be my best interests. He later confessed that he was concerned that if I became a Christian, I might go the whole way and become a preacher! My dad was quite astute to be fair.

I did not want to rock the boat with my family. My dad had told me that, when I completed university, there was a chance of me getting involved in his business. This would have secured a decent life for me – a house, a car, money etc. I thought it would be best to wait until I had all these material trappings, then I could think about becoming a Christian. It didn't quite work out that way.

I went to my bed that night, but I could not get to sleep. A thought kept on coming into my mind, "You can have a house, a car, money – but you can't take them with you when you die – and you don't know when that's going to be". I later discovered that this sentence was a paraphrase of a Bible verse that says, "And what do you benefit if you gain the whole world but lose your own soul?"

I tossed and turned – deep down I knew that I had found what I was looking for, where I least expected it and when I least felt I needed it. I did not have a clue how to pray or become a Christian. I simply said, "Over to you God".

I must have fallen asleep almost immediately after that simple prayer. I woke up the next morning, and the only way I can describe how I felt was that something inside me had come alive. God was real to me. I found a New Testament in one of my drawers. When I was in second year at Largs Academy, two suited men came to one of our assemblies, calling themselves Gideons. This is an organisation that gives out free New Testaments. One of the Gideons was called Mr Smellie. This may sound strange, but I had so much respect for this man telling a group of second year pupils what his real name was that I listened to him! He told this story of two sons who were given a choice by their father. They could have £5 or a New Testament. I was thinking, "I would go for the fiver." One son did opt for the fiver but the other boy chose the New Testament and when he opened it there was £5 inside every page. His dad was trying to teach him the value of the Bible. Anyway, when Mr Smellie finished telling this story and asked who would like to receive a testament, I was right down at the front of the assembly hall to receive one – hoping to find it filled with fivers. Of course, it wasn't, but it was a good story.

I put the little book away in a drawer and thought nothing of it, until the morning after I had handed my life over to Jesus. When I read it, the words seemed to come alive and make sense.

As I began my spiritual journey, I was determined not to kiss my brains goodbye. I am very wary of any belief system that dissuades its followers from asking hard questions. Having opened up my life to Jesus, I wanted to objectively examine all the evidence about who he was, why he died and whether he really did rise again from the dead as Christians claim.

I became convinced that someone called Jesus, who came from Nazereth, existed and was put to death by the Romans. It seems clear, even to secular historians, that Jesus was put to death because he made claims that he was God in human form – claims that the religious leaders of his day considered blasphemous. I thought that Jesus had to be psychotic, a psychopath or the real deal. Let me explain.

His family actually did think he was psychotic, that he experienced delusions. If you put yourself in their shoes, it is understandable. At the age of 30, he turned to his siblings and said, "You are actually my *step* brothers and sisters, we share the same mother but not the same father. My dad is God!" Let's face it, in psychiatric units today there are many people who think they are the Son of God.

Or maybe he was a psychopath and he knew exactly what he was doing? Was he duping people into following him so that he could control, manipulate and exploit them and then let them die as martyrs?

Neither of these scenarios seemed probable to me, so I saw no other option other than that he was who he said he was – God in human form. Worth getting to know in that case!

And what about that horrific death on the cross? In football we use a phrase, "taking one for the team." It refers to a player who deliberately commits a foul in order to stop an opponent getting past him into a goalscoring position. He knows he will probably be booked or sent off, but he sacrifices himself for the sake of his team. Jesus "took one for the team" but the only person who suffered was him. It's perhaps not the best analogy of Jesus' death on the cross because he did not commit "a foul". He did nothing wrong throughout his entire life. In fact, he was taking the punishment on himself for all the wrong things that everyone else has done. Jesus was our substitute.

Let me illustrate this further. The story is told of two people who went through school and university together and became close friends. Later in life they lost contact. One became a criminal and the other a judge. One day the criminal appeared before the judge, pleading guilty to a crime he had committed. The judge recognised his former friend but had a dilemma. He was a judge so he had to be fair. He could not let his friend off with what he had done. He did not want to punish him either because he loved him. He gave him the correct penalty and announced his fine. He then stepped down, took off his judge's wig and wrote a cheque for the amount of the fine. The judge paid the penalty for his friend because he loved him. That's what Jesus did for us when he died on the cross. We simply need to cash the cheque by asking Jesus to forgive us and come into our life to lead us.

However, if Jesus died and that was the end of him, I did wonder what good he could possibly do today. The Bible claims that three days after his death, Jesus rose again, and over a period of 40 days, he appeared to people on 12 occasions. I looked at all the evidence surrounding the claims for the resurrection of Jesus and became utterly convinced it had happened as the Bible had outlined. What ultimately convinced me was the change in Jesus' disciples from before his crucifixion to after his resurrection. As Jesus was being arrested, all of them kept their distance from him, and Peter even denied that he knew him. However, they were so convinced that they had seen, talked with and even touched Jesus after his resurrection that most of them died as martyrs because they refused to refute their claim that he had risen again. In my experience, people usually lie to get *out* of trouble, not to get *in* to trouble. That was it. I am an "all in or all out" type of person. I was in!

However, the change in my life was gradual. My first attempt at sharing my new-found faith did not go particularly well. I decided to tell my mate, Gus, because I thought he was the least likely to laugh at me. Here is how the conversation went:

"Gus, mate, I've something important to tell you."

"Sounds serious, wee man, what is it?"

"Well, I've become a Christian."

Gus was doubled over laughing for about 30 seconds before replying.

"That's the best wind up you've ever come out with. Brilliant, wee man, brilliant."

"Mate, I'm actually being serious, I have become a Christian, honest!"

"Aye, so you have. Away you go, ya wee wind up merchant…"

"Look, I ****** have become a ****** Christian right…"

I know what you're thinking, not very appropriate language for a Christian to use, and you are right. It does perhaps explains why I got on so well with John Lambie though. Eventually, I cleaned up my language, however, I still found it very difficult to convince people that I had genuinely given my life to Jesus.

The next person I decided to tell was Mrs Urquhart, who had been my French teacher at school. She was a lovely Christian lady and I was sure that she would be delighted to hear about my new-found faith. By this time I had left school, but I went in to see her to relay my good news. Her response? "Oh Mark – away with you! Get out of my classroom you wee rascal." Like Gus, she too thought I was winding her up!

A few weeks later, I came across some books I had procured from the school before I left – okay I had stolen them. I decided to send them back to the school via my neighbour, Cameron, who was still a pupil. I told him to take them to Mrs Urquhart, and I enclosed a letter, which read, "Dear Mrs Urquhart, as I told you, I've given my life to Jesus and recently I was reminded of books I had stolen from school and I want to return them with my apologies."

I received a lovely reply, "Dear Mark, now I believe! I'm so happy for you too!" God has a sense of humour – her son Neil was the first chaplain I appointed, when I placed him at Kilmarnock.

The biggest difference others noticed in me was that I used to be quite bad tempered and get into lots of fights. Now, I found myself viewing and treating people with much more compassion. A perfect example of this was a girl who I used to detest as a young boy, though I should point out this never led to a physical altercation – she would have beat me up anyway. I was in constant conflict with her, largely because her best friend was also my girlfriend – okay I was only eight years old but I'm telling you – we were in love! This other girl was the proverbial gooseberry, always getting in the way. My girlfriend and I gradually drifted apart, but I was still sad when she moved to Blackpool at the age of 13. However, this was offset by the joy I had at seeing my arch nemesis move away at the same time to North Berwick.

When I became a Christian at the age of 16, the first church I went to was probably not the best choice for me. No one seemed to share my enthusiasm about Jesus! Then, one person suggested I meet this other girl in the church who was into that "Jesus stuff". The girl had recently moved back to the village from, you guessed it, North Berwick!

When I saw my former enemy I could not believe my eyes, yet, I have to say, we bonded immediately. Now, before you start thinking this person was Aileen and suggest this would make a great plot for a chick flick, let me burst your bubble. Romance would never stand a chance of blossoming between us. She was much taller than me and I would not have liked to have had a constant crick in my neck. We did become the best of friends, however, and I conducted Mairi's wedding some years' later. It was on top of a Munro mountain, Stob Ghabar.

The following week at the wedding reception, I started speaking to her brother Allan Cowan, who had led the Save the Jags campaign. However, I have already told you that story. God works in mysterious ways!

Ever since I invited Jesus into my life, I have been on an incredible spiritual journey with God. I have been utterly amazed at how his plan for my life has unfolded, my life could not be in better hands. As a teenager, if you had told me that I would become a wholehearted follower of Jesus and a football chaplain, I would have laughed as much as everyone else did when I first told them I had actually become a Christian!

CHAPTER 21

CHURCHES AND FOOTBALL CLUBS –
AN UNLIKELY PARTNERSHIP?

The development of football chaplaincy in Scotland has been a challenging path to navigate, partly because of historic sectarianism in Scotland and also because of the cultural distance between churches and football clubs. It is, however, a very different story in England.

Many of England's top football clubs were started by churches during the Victorian era. People moved away from the country's rural areas into the burgeoning urbanised communities. Many churches in large towns and cities felt they were losing touch with their local community, so they thought it would be a good idea to form a sports club, particularly to engage with young men.

One such example was Aston Villa in Birmingham, which was birthed out of a young men's Bible class in 1874. It was actually first named Aston Villa Wesleyan Football Club. Rev Charles Beecroft, a Methodist minister, was appointed as its first president in 1877.

Other clubs known to have been started by a church during that period are: Barnsley, Birmingham City, Bolton Wanderers, Everton, Fulham, Queens Park Rangers, Southampton, Swindon Town and Tottenham Hotspur.

My favourite story of that time is about a vicar's daughter, Anna Connell, who lived in an impoverished inner city area. She wanted to start a football club to encourage local young men to pursue healthy pastimes, rather than drinking too much alcohol and "causing trouble". When she started the team in 1880, they played on a piece of waste land. It turns out they were pretty good… Today they are called Manchester City! The Blue half of Manchester owes a great debt to Anna Connell. She is believed to be the only woman in the world to have founded a male professional football club.

The first organised association football league in the world is the English Football League. It was founded in 1888 by a well-respected Christian Scotsman, William McGregor. He had been a member of the committee at Aston Villa since 1877, fulfilling the roles of president, director and chairman. William had become frustrated because a number of Villa's games had been cancelled and so he wanted to bring better organisation to the game in England. He gathered together representatives from the country's top clubs, they formed the Football League, and member clubs were given a guaranteed fixture list each season. So it's fair to say that churches and individual Christians played a pivotal role in the development of English football, even though those links lessened as the game developed into a professional sport.

It's a different story in Scotland. In fact, only two clubs appear to have been started by a church – in both cases, Roman Catholic churches – Glasgow Celtic and Hibernian. It could be argued that another major Scottish club has similar roots. Dundee Hibernian was started in 1909 by the local Irish Catholic community, inspired by the example of their Edinburgh counterparts. However, in 1923 their name was changed by a group of local businessmen who wanted to appeal to a wider audience than the local Catholic community. Ever since then, the club has been known as Dundee United.

Glasgow Rangers has historically been seen as the Protestant club of Scotland but this label has been more about setting them apart from Celtic, their major rivals, who had a predominantly Catholic support. Until Maurice Johnston signed for Rangers in 1989, the club had never knowingly signed a Roman Catholic. At the time, Johnston's signing caused quite a stir among sections of the Rangers support. However, most of the animosity shown towards wee Mo was assuaged when he began to score goals for his team, especially when he hit the back of the net against Celtic. Rangers have signed many Catholics since then. Celtic have always had a policy of signing Protestants and Catholics. Although in 1895, there was a resolution suggesting that the team introduce a limit on the number of Protestants allowed into the team. This was rejected and the club has since remained open to all faiths.

Sectarianism remains an issue in Scottish football. For that reason, we always make it clear that a chaplain's church is no more connected to the football club than the club doctor's medical practice. Understandably, most Scottish teams do not want to be identified as Protestant or Catholic, so none of our chaplains would identify themselves as either. They simply define themselves as Christian and there is a wide variety of church backgrounds among them.

Historically, the Protestant Church in Scotland has had a reputation of being stern. Football was possibly viewed as a distraction from spiritual matters.

When I became a church pastor in 1988, I witnessed this attitude first-hand. My visit to a retired leader from the church remains ones of my funniest recollections during my 10 years in Paisley. At least, it was funny to me.

He did nothing but moan about the church and how standards had slipped, leading to moral compromise. He said, "I'll tell you how bad things are getting. Just last week I saw a deacon from the Baptist Church coming out of Love Street [home of St Mirren]. What do you think of that?" Obviously, the look on my face gave away the fact that I could not see anything wrong with it. He asked me, "You don't go to watch football do you?" Wanting to lighten the situation with a bit of banter, I replied, "Well, no, not exactly. I support Partick Thistle…"

He was horrified. "But what about all that bad language you hear? How can you as a Christian listen to that?" I replied, "To be honest I'd hear just as bad language walking down Paisley High Street. Anyway, there's not that many people go to Thistle games so I could be sitting somewhere where I don't so much as hear a dog bark outside the ground on Firhill Road!"

He was not satisfied with my response. If you have had a strict, legalistic church upbringing, you may be able to relate to his final challenge. Speaking in sober tones, he said, "Well young man, let me ask you this…

CONFESSIONS OF A FOOTBALL CHAPLAIN

How would you feel if, at half-time, Jesus Christ was to return, and there you were, sitting at a football match? Well, how would you feel about that?" I responded, "Well, to be honest, there have been some games recently when things have being going so badly, the thought of Jesus returning at half-time and getting me out of there sounds brilliant!" Suffice to say, he did not find my quip particularly funny.

Churches reflecting this man's viewpoint are dying out and I do not think any will survive beyond my life time. However, churches that positively engage with their communities, including their local football clubs, are growing. Our church in Kilsyth changed its name from Kilsyth Congregational Church to Kilsyth Community Church in order to communicate that we did not exist merely for our own benefit. We wanted to be a positive influence in our community. Because we were known locally as KCC, when the local newspaper reported on our name change, they wrote that we were "still the same but different". Somehow, Graham Norton picked up on this headline on his TV show and, as well as making light of us, hilariously suggested ways in which we could "be the same but different". A decent PR exercise for KCC.

Over the years, quite a number of players and managers have asked to come along to my church in Kilsyth. They were always made very welcome. They thoroughly enjoyed the lively worship music from our band but I'm not so sure what they thought of the wee preacher... However, not all players felt comfortable about coming into a church building. The next story illustrates that well.

Two years after conducting his wedding, Jamie Mitchell asked me, "Rev, do you christen weans?" I replied, "Well kind of… I believe that God has created your little one, and designed her to be a genius at something. I could conduct a blessing service for her whereby I would pray that the full potential that God has placed within her will be released so that she lives out her God-given dreams." I was not sure if that made any sense, but he seemed to like the sound of it.

I invited him to our church for the blessing service. Now, he was not so sure! "The thing is Rev, I don't live that close to the church, and probably wouldn't likely be back there. I'd feel like I was just using the church. Would you consider coming to our house to do it and we'll just have family and friends round?" I said that I understood and would be delighted to do that.

However, by the following week there had been a development. Jamie said that he wanted all the players to come to the blessing too. Would I mind if the venue was changed to a function suite at Tiger Tiger, a well-known nightclub in Glasgow? I did not have to think twice! In fact, I suggested that I bring our church worship band, our street dance team and our puppet team, and provide church at Tiger Tiger. Jamie was delighted with my offer.

What a night it was! Everyone was surprised at the quality of the music, dancing and puppets. More than that, they were happy to listen to the message that was shared through these means as well as what I had to say.

CONFESSIONS OF A FOOTBALL CHAPLAIN

At the end of the evening, I was standing at the bar talking to one of our players. He said something to me that I will never forget, "That was brilliant Rev. Really got me thinking. You know, I've never been able to make a connection between you and the church before tonight, because, like, you're alright"!

Makes you think doesn't it? Scottish people for the most part have a negative impression of Christians and churches, exacerbated in part by our portrayal in the media, but also by how we have presented ourselves in the past. I do not want the chaplain to be seen as a religious authority figure, someone who is going to lecture people about their language or lifestyle. We are servants of the football clubs at which we work. We have no agenda other than to make a positive difference to our clubs.

A footballer or manager's value is generally based on their performance and results. You can turn from being a hero to "a zero" within seconds. Because our role is not performance-based, chaplains value people in a different way. We seek to view people the way we are viewed by God. I don't believe that God loves me because of my religious performance or the spiritual results I produce, He loves me unconditionally. Chaplains seek to demonstrate how much God unconditionally loves and values everyone through how *we* treat them.

At the beginning of the book, I spoke of my love for Partick Thistle and how chaplaincy became my way of making a positive contribution to the club. That same desire remains part of the DNA of Sports Chaplaincy

Scotland. Chaplains seek to have a constructive impact on the lives of all those who contribute to the "beautiful game".

I have written a lot about the benefits that chaplaincy can bring to football clubs. However, it is also right to point out that churches have so much to learn from working in partnership with these clubs. It's a two way street. Churches can help football clubs build bridges into their communities and vice-versa. Our Dundee chaplain, Michael Holloway, was asked to speak at an assembly of senior pupils in the school at which he is chaplain. He brought two of the Dens Park players with him. It was a good opportunity for the club as they are competing for local support, given their rivals, United, are literally across the road from Dundee's stadium. It was also a good exercise for Michael, because the pupils now thought he was pretty cool, having mates who were footballers!

Sports Chaplaincy Scotland and Scottish football have worked together to great effect, leaving a wonderful legacy in a country that might surprise you – Rwanda. The country is well known for its horrific genocide of 1994, when around one million Tutsi and moderate Hutu people were murdered in one hundred days.

After the First World War, Belgium became the colonial rulers of Rwanda. At that time Rwanda was comprised of three tribes – Tutsi (14%), Hutu (85%) and the Pygmy Twa (1%). The Belgians used the Tutsi to rule the country and gave them many privileges that the Hutu were denied, including western-style education and political power.

Racial identification cards were also distributed, which identified if the citizens of Rwanda were Hutu or Tutsi. In 1956, the Tutsi leaders called for independence from Belgium and this caused Rwanda's colonial occupiers to switch allegiance to the Hutu majority. The resentment and anger of the Hutu, fuelled by extremists, culminated in an attempt to exterminate the entire Tutsi population of Rwanda, beginning on 7 April 1994. When the genocide started, most white people abandoned the country, leaving the Tutsi to their fate.

In the aftermath of the genocide, there could have been the potential for ongoing recriminations. However, the new government decided on a policy that saw the rejection of tribal distinctions, so that everyone was to declare themselves to be simply Rwandan. Over the years, through healing and reconciliation projects, many of which were instigated by churches, the country has made a remarkable recovery. Many former perpetrators of the genocide have repented of their killings and sought to help rebuild the lives of survivors through house-building and agricultural projects. Many survivors have forgiven perpetrators who murdered their families and have been willing to rebuild their community alongside their former enemies.

In 2008, I was introduced to this beautiful country by the charity, Comfort International. It is not an understatement to say that, as a result of that first trip, I fell in love with the Rwandan people and I knew I had formed lasting relationships with my new friends. I have been going there nearly every year since. Generally speaking, in my experience, the Rwandans are humble, gentle, gracious and so friendly.

I now consider Rwanda as my second home. Since 2011, I have appreciated any opportunity to lead a group of Scottish people to the "land of a thousand hills", so they can experience for themselves what a wonderful transformation has taken place in the people of this country. In 2015, I was helping to lead a group of school pupils from Kilsyth Academy. On this visit, I became good friends with Jacques Kayisire, a former Rwandan professional footballer. He had survived the genocide through the intervention of Hutu teammates. They protected him from Genocidaires at the risk of their own lives. Desiring to give something back to Rwandan football, he started the Dream Team Youth Football Academy in Kigali, the capital city. His aim was to develop not only football skills, but also life skills of children and teenagers. As Jacques and I talked, we began to dream of the possibility of bringing football coaches from Scotland to Rwanda.

Meanwhile back in Scotland, during the 2014 Glasgow Commonwealth Games, the Rwandan team was hosted by East Lothian Council. Great relationships were formed between their respective leaders. The Council was keen to continue their relationship with their new Rwandan friends. One of the suggestions put forward was for a group of coaches from Tranent Colts Community Football Club to visit Rwanda. It was just a case of finding someone who led groups to the country and had good football contacts. I wonder who that could be?

In June 2016, I took nine coaches from Tranent to Rwanda. I also brought two coaches from the Scottish FA – Sean McCauley and Alan White (commonly known as Chalky). Sean is also a coach at Bonnyrigg

CONFESSIONS OF A FOOTBALL CHAPLAIN

Rose, and Chalky is Hearts' Head of Community. One of our chaplains, Kiki, then at Fort William, also came on the trip with his son Donald. The group were awestruck at how Rwanda has recovered from the terrible genocide of 1994. They were astounded at the countless stories they heard from Rwandan people who had been enabled by God to forgive the killers who had murdered their families. All the coaches commented that if they could embrace such incredible reconciliation in Rwanda, surely we could defeat sectarianism in Scotland.

The Rwandan people we met were *equally* blown away by the sacrificial kindness of the football coaches. The group enjoyed working with local churches that were engaged in projects to give food and shelter to homeless children. Jacques organised for over 20 local youth football team coaches to come together to learn how the Tranent coaches ran a community football club with volunteers and limited resources – something to which the Rwandans could aspire.

Chalky and Sean explained about the coach education pathway in Scotland, and began to explore the possibility of delivering a similar programme in Rwanda on a future trip. The Scottish FA had given me a substantial amount of training kit, which we were able to distribute to the Rwandan coaches. Tranent Colts had also brought surplus kit and football boots, which were given to the numerous children they coached. The highlight of the trip for the Scots was delivering coaching to the children from the supported needs school, next door to our Guest House. I was so impressed at how the Scottish coaches adapted to the local culture. For example, one of the main lessons learned in Rwanda was summed up by the most quoted phrase on the trip, "Guys, there's been a change of plan…" Let's just say that we had to be very flexible in the timing and make-up of the activities we planned.

Such was the impact of the visit to Rwanda on the Scottish group, in February 2020, Heart of Midlothian helped facilitate Chalky and I to organise another trip. Phil, Mike and Allan from Tranent came back to Rwanda with us, and were joined by coaches from Bonnyrigg Rose, Spartans, Penicuik Athletic, Murieston United and Ormiston. Chalky also brought fellow Scottish FA coach, Jack Beesley, who also plays for Broxburn Athletic.

Chalky and Jack agreed to provide coach education for a maximum of 30 and a minimum of 16 local football coaches, through my friend Jacques Kayisire. Even up until the week before we arrived in Rwanda, we were concerned that Jacques was not going to be able to gather enough coaches to make the course viable.

We need not have worried – 56 turned up! And not just from Rwanda. Interpreters were needed for those who had arrived from DR Congo, Uganda and Kenya. Chalky and Jack were concerned that everyone had been able to understand what they were teaching. However, on the final day when the African coaches had to deliver coaching sessions based on what they had learned, the Scottish educators were amazed at the quality on display from their students.

The rest of the Scottish group gave of their time in coaching children from many different youth teams, and of course, the children from the supported needs school next door to our Guest House. They also brought over invaluable football equipment to help support the Rwandan youth coaches. We flew with Turkish Airlines and they kindly gifted us an extra 150 kg of luggage allowance on top of the 40kg each that we already had – and we needed it! The group donated full sets of football kit to 10 different youth teams. They brought a variety of football equipment and an abundance of toiletries and clothing – items that we would probably take for granted in Scotland. Yet, most of the group felt that Rwanda had more of a positive effect on them than they had on Rwanda. The friendly welcome, appreciation, love, and kindness they received from the Rwandans has left every one of them wanting to go back again. It was such a great example of how churches and football clubs can work together to make a positive difference in their local communities.

Since then, a charity, "Scottish Football for Rwanda" has been formed with a view to developing coaching connections and charitable work and it is my privilege to be chairman of this group. If we can do something like this in Rwanda, there is no reason why we cannot develop working together in Scotland.

The industry of professional football can be ruthless and brutal, but most of the people I have worked with within the game are quite the opposite. Yes, I know that the lack of money to go round everyone in the national game can sometimes lead to in-fighting. Yet, I have found the Scottish football family to be full of kind-hearted people who want to positively impact their local community – just as churches do.

An unlikely partnership? Probably, but it is a relationship that I have thoroughly enjoyed pioneering and I look forward to us journeying together in the future. In the words of one of my favourite sayings, "The best is yet to come!"

CONFESSIONS OF A FOOTBALL CHAPLAIN

AFTERWORD BY DANNY LENNON

I love football. To me it is the beautiful game. It is a theme that has run through my whole life and I am very grateful for that. Playing and winning a good game are some of the most satisfying and rewarding feelings in the world. However, football both gives and takes in our life. It has given me great memories as I have pursued my dreams and seen many of them come true, but that has come at a cost at times. A life in football has taken me away from my loved ones more than I would like, it has required tough choices to be made, it has taken away my privacy and opened me up to an incredible amount of pressure and very public criticism.

The emotional rollercoaster and its never ending procession of challenges is a big part of the reason we love football so much, but it can also overwhelm you at times. Whilst football gives and takes from us, Mark Fleming and his nationwide team of sports chaplains are very much the good guys, in that they only ever give and never take. They are an invaluable support and never seek praise or thanks.

In my time as a player Mark was often the sensible voice of reason as well as a practical support for me and many of my teammates. His care and relationship with us helped us to perform better not only on the pitch, but also as ambassadors for our club and in our personal lives.

As a manager, I began to realise very quickly that man management requires you to be different things to different people, in order to bring the best out of them. At times you need to be a role model and a leader,

... at other times you have to be a father figure or a friend. For some you need to be a headmaster and a boss, then to others you are an agony aunt or a therapist. No one can be all things to all people. This is where Mark and his chaplains come into their own. They are skilled listeners, well versed in pastoral care. They are compassionate and motivated to really, truly help. They have a wealth of contacts that I have tapped into over the years to help players overcome addictions, financial issues, mental health problems, relationship difficulties and bereavement. They have, time and time again, helped people to unburden themselves and perform at their best.

My relationship with Mark is one for which I am eternally grateful. He has helped me to enjoy my journey in football to the full. More especially, he has helped me to realise and appreciate that my identity is not found in football, but that I am a husband, a father, a son, a friend and a child of God, who enjoys having football as part of my life. That perspective is key.

I am glad you have had the opportunity to read Mark's book. I hope and pray you get an opportunity to meet the man himself in person. I also hope and pray you get to meet the one whom Mark loves and serves with all that he has got. In the words of Liverpool manager, Jurgen Klopp, "Jesus is the most important person who ever lived and incredibly, he is alive today." My relationship with Jesus is such a comfort to me, an inspiration and a source of strength. That relationship is available to everyone, all you need to do is ask for it and it will be given.

I wish you every success in football and in life. May God richly bless you.

CONFESSIONS OF A FOOTBALL CHAPLAIN

ACKNOWLEDGEMENTS

COVID-19 and the resultant lockdown measures have had a different impact on all of us. The crisis has brought a mix of grief, loss, stress and anxiety but it has also provided an opportunity for some people to reflect on what is important and to engage in activities that they would not normally have time for. Lockdown gave me the time to write this book so I'm grateful for that.

My thanks go to every person referred to within these pages, not only for their contribution to this book, but also for their contribution to Scottish football in general.

I firstly want to thank my wife Aileen. She has never been a football supporter but she has given me unwavering support, help and encouragement as I have developed chaplaincy in Scottish football. Back in 1983, when I asked her dad, Bob, for her hand in marriage, he jokingly said, "Well, you ken what she's like son – if that's what you want then go ahead!" The truth is, neither of us really knew what we were letting ourselves in for. Yet, anyone who knows us as a couple, will tell you that Aileen is the one who deserves an award for being able to navigate through life with me. She truly does have the patience of a saint! Aileen has nearly 40 years' experience of bringing correction to me so it was only natural to invite her to be one of my proof readers. She knows me well and claims that she always knows what I am thinking so she was able to help me explain myself when I was struggling for the right words.

Keeping it in the family, I also want to thank my eldest daughter Kirsty. She spent a lot of time going over the book with a fine tooth comb and was immensely helpful with grammar and sentence construction. Quite how my youngest daughter Bethany found time to proof read the book, while looking after my two adorable grandsons, Isaac and Noah, is beyond me. Having such a supportive husband in James must surely have helped. I'm grateful to her for all the helpful suggestions and encouragement.

My dear friend Janice Straiton holds an English Literature degree and as well as helping with grammar, she, along with my other proof readers, kept me in the realm of political correctness. So if anyone *was* offended by anything I have written, just be thankful to these four people because you are likely to have been even *more* offended if they had not intervened!

I thought it would be a good idea to ask for editing input from two friends who have worked as sports journalists and one who is still working in this field. Our chaplain to Queen's Park Women, Lorna Farrell, is a former presenter at ITV, has written for several national newspapers and is a regular contributor on BBC Radio. She is also the former Head of Sport at Scot FM and Real Radio – well used to working in a football environment. She read the first draft and suggested some very helpful changes so that the book would be understood and enjoyed by anyone, including those who do not have a faith background or a knowledge of football.

CONFESSIONS OF A FOOTBALL CHAPLAIN

My friend Iain King is former Head of Sport at the Scottish Sun. Iain was Scottish Sports Writer of the Year for an unprecedented three successive years (2006, 2007 and 2008) and has written six excellent books on different footballers. I asked him to assess the book and I am very grateful to him for his invaluable input and advice.

Alan Campbell is a freelance sports reporter for whom I have the utmost respect. At times he has been a lone voice crying out in the wilderness of Scottish football journalism, as he has sought to highlight and promote the female game in our country. I am thankful to Alan for providing me with invaluable information, thus helping me give women's football the recognition it deserves.

Confidentiality is an essential value of chaplaincy so this was never going to be a kiss and tell book. The challenge was, how do I tell hilarious stories, particularly from my time as chaplain to Partick Thistle, without incriminating individuals or breaking trust? So, I phoned round a number of former Jags players to ask for their permission to include funny recollections about them in the book. Surprisingly, every single player I contacted was happy for me to name them and share any details that I wanted – now, *that* is trust! I must admit, in every conversation I cried with laughter as we reminisced about some of the Firhill shenanigans. In particular my thanks go to Danny Lennon, Scott McLean, Kenny Arthur, Mark Roberts, George Shaw, Gerry Britton and Chic Charnley who provided much of the hilarity in these pages at their own expense.

CONFESSIONS OF A FOOTBALL CHAPLAIN

Though I can no longer thank him personally, special acknowledgement should be given to my great friend – the late John Lambie. He was one of the most colourful Scottish football managers ever – and that was just his language! Despite my persistent encouragement, John refused to write a book about his experiences in football because he felt he would need to be honest about instances where he had been badly treated and he did not want to paint anyone in a negative light. I promised him that one day I would write a book and when I did, he would feature heavily in it – though I have not incriminated anyone who mistreated him. He was delighted with the prospect of me doing this and regaled me with many outrageous stories of his time in football. However, I think he forgot it was a chaplain who would be writing the book so there are some stories he told me that I have chosen to take to the grave with me!

I would also like to thank our many chaplains throughout Scottish football who have contributed to these pages with their funny stories, usually involving laughing at themselves. If the image of a chaplain is a sombre individual then I hope this book has blown that idea out of the water for you.

That said, there are some sad stories within these pages that I hope you found moving and also illuminating in terms of the vital work the chaplains do. The reason why chaplaincy has grown so much in Scottish football is not because I am a great salesman but because the chaplains have such a great reputation for serving their respective clubs so well.

The appearance of a book can have a significant influence on whether someone picks it up to have a read, especially if they don't know the author. So a big thank you to Stuart Polson, who is responsible for the graphic design of the book cover.

My thanks go to Craig Brown, the most successful ever manager of the Scotland Men's National Team, for writing the foreword. Craig is the esteemed patron of Sports Chaplaincy Scotland and a great advocate of chaplaincy within football. He has spoken at many events on our behalf and I never tire of hearing his hilarious stories from the period when he managed Scotland. I have not included any of those accounts but I hope you enjoyed his "chaplain story" when he was manager of Preston North End – it's a belter!

Not only has Danny Lennon provided me with some side-splitting material from his playing days at Partick Thistle, he has also been one of my best friends in the game. I asked him to write the afterword because he is well-placed to sum up the benefits of chaplaincy, having made good use of the service throughout his career.

Having asked Craig to write a foreword and Danny an afterword, I was also keen to include input from my friend Eddie Wolecki Black. He has experienced the benefits of chaplaincy as a manager in both men's and women's football. Our mutual friend Iain King, therefore, suggested that Eddie wrote a "middleword" on his experiences of football chaplaincy and I decided to place that, unsurprisingly, somewhere in the middle of the book!

CONFESSIONS OF A FOOTBALL CHAPLAIN

I am grateful to have had the privilege of serving three Scottish football clubs as a chaplain - Partick Thistle, Hibernian Women and Bonnyrigg Rose Athletic. It has also been a great privilege to serve as chaplain to the Scottish FA. All these experiences have given me a broad and invaluable insight into various levels of the game in Scotland.

Last but most certainly not least, I thank God who has done more for me and through me than I could ever have asked or imagined. I hope you are able to see the ways in which he has worked for the benefit of those involved in the beautiful game in Scotland and that you have also received an understanding of how much he loves you personally.

Printed in Great Britain
by Amazon